MW00414762

The Walker Sisters:
Spirited Women of the Smokies

Estette M Cardone
from

Dear Hubby Bill Cardone
Christmas 2006
(Also Elizabeth's First Christmas)
with us

By

Bonnie Trentham Myers

With Lynda Myers Boyer

The Walker Sisters:
Spirited Women of the Smokies

Copyright © 2004

ISBN 0-9727839-3-8

Myers & Myers Publishers
2112 Sentell Circle
Maryville, TN 37803

Myersbon@AOL.com
GlennMyers@BellSouth.net
LMBoyer@AOL.com

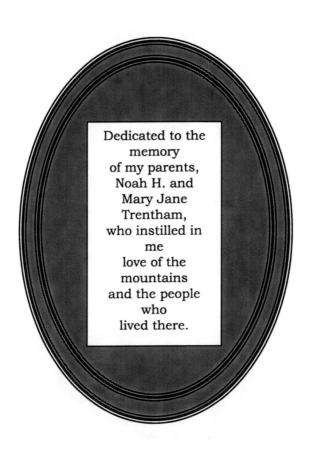

Dedicated to the
memory
of my parents,
Noah H. and
Mary Jane
Trentham,
who instilled in
me
love of the
mountains
and the people
who
lived there.

MY MOUNTAIN HOME

By
Louisa Walker
(Original spelling retained)

There is an old weather bettion house
That stands near a wood
With an orchard near by it
For all most one hundred years it has stood.

It was my home from infancy
It sheltered me in youth
When I tell you I love it
I tell you the truth.

For years it has sheltered
By day and by night
From the summer sun's heat
And the cold winter blight.

But now the park commesser
Comes all dressed up so gay
Saying this old house of yours
We must now take away.

They coax and they weedle
They fret and they bark
Saying we have to have this place
For a national park.

For us poor mountain people
They don't have a care
But must a home for
The wolf the lion and the bear

But many of us have a title
That is sure and will hold
To the City of peace
Where the streets are pure gold.

There no lion in its fury
Those pathes ever trod
It is the house of the soul
In the presence of God

When we reach the portles
Of glory so fair'
The wolf cannot enter
Neither the lion or bear.

And no park commissioner
Will ever dar
To desturbe or molest
Or take our home from us there.

Used with permission of the Walker Sisters' niece,
Effie Phipps (daughter of Caroline and Jim Shelton.)
Other poems found at the end of the book.

Acknowledgements

I could not undertake a project of this type without the help of many people. I was fortunate to have the opportunity to interview many who knew and loved the Walker Sisters. Some were relatives. Some were friends. Some gave me information I have not found anywhere else. All were personally acquainted with the life and times of the Walker Sisters and have discussed at length many of the topics included in this book.

I sincerely thank those who took their time to allow me to interview them and those who allowed me to use materials they held. With special thanks to Glenn Cardwell, Dwight McCarter, Lucinda Ogle, Herb Clabo, Ralph Patty, Lendel Abbott, Gladys Fogerty, Maryann Neubert, Effie Phipps (Walker Sisters' niece, daughter of Caroline and Jim Shelton.), Fred Walker (Walker Sisters' nephew, son of John Henry), and Myrtle Walker Trentham, his sister. I particularly want to thank the delightful Robin (Mrs. Jim) Goddard. Mrs. Goddard spent many nights in the Walker Sisters' home as she and Elsie Burrell helped with many chores including making ice cream and drying apples.

TABLE OF CONTENT

The Walker Sisters:
Front L to R- Margaret, Louisa, Polly
Back L to R- Hettie, Martha, Nancy, Caroline
Courtesy of Effie Phipps

INTRODUCTION

The Walker Sisters were perhaps more famous for what they did not do than for what they did. Because of an article in the Saturday Evening Post April 27, 1946, thousands of tourists beat a path to their door. The article described the quaint existence of five sisters who chose to remain in their split-log home in the Great Smoky Mountains National Park rather than to move to modern housing outside the Park. The article suggested that if you were curious about how your great-great grandfather lived, raising his own food and producing his own clothing, you would find that life here in these Tennessee hills.

If most of us were compelled today to use a mattock to plant and cultivate all the food we eat, as these sisters did, we would likely starve. Their life style was unlike any the rest of us knew. Their parents had trained them well. They had ingrained a stoic determination and stubbornness. These sisters thrived in a harsh setting. In addition, they were decent, peaceful, law-abiding citizens. If you have an almost perfect situation, the article suggested, why improve on it?

The Saturday Evening Post article changed their lives as it also introduced many to their way of life. At first, the sisters put up a sign saying "Keep Out." When they began to sell apples, pine cones, fried apple pies, lye soap, coverlets, toys such as tops and whimmy-diddles, and the poems that Louisa wrote, they changed the sign to read "Visitors Welcome." One wag said they lived off tourists in summer and " 'taters in winter."

These women were born in a very remote area of Sevier County, Tennessee, in which Little Greenbriar Cove is located. Many considered this area one of the most isolated in the southeastern United States. Abraham Lincoln reportedly pointed to an area map and commented on the tremendous need for educational advantages in the region. Some say this is the reason Lincoln Memorial University is located at Harrogate, Tennessee today.

Their neighbors, including my family, agreed to sell their property to the U.S. Park Service in the 1930's. These neighbors purchased houses, cars, radios, and electrical appliances. Except for one sister who married, the Walker Sisters continued to work a 122-acre farm exactly as their parents and grandparents had done--without electricity, gasoline engines, running water, or toilet facilities. Nancy Melinda, who died in 1931, did not experience the coming of the Park. However, the other five sisters remained in their home until the last sister, Louisa Susan, died in 1964. By 1953 only two sisters, Margaret Jane (aged 83) and Louisa (aged 71) remained. At that time, they asked the park superintendent to remove the sign on Highway 73 directing tourists to their home.

They were not eccentric or illiterate. They chose what was most comfortable for them. It is important to discuss their lives in the context of the community in which they lived. Even though they did not experience life in the same way most of us experienced it, life outside their mountain home influenced their existence. Ideas, inventions, and people affected them even if only to consider and refuse to accept them. They did not forgo all modern conveniences. They rode with friends and relatives in cars. They adopted newer methods of farming. They were very reluctant, however, to make changes that were very different to a life they knew as young women.

Their choice ordained a lifestyle that was more in line with life in the 18th or 19th century. Luxuries were scarce, but the girls considered them useless or sinful. Life for the Walker family was never easy. However, they survived with love and laughter, pride and honor. The Walker Sisters' isolation, no doubt, helped to determine their attitudes toward the rest of the world. However, they were not generally troubled with world affairs. They did not pay electric, telephone, water, or sewer bills. They did not experience the Great Depression with its bank closings and mortgage foreclosures as most Americans did. In fact, they did not trust banks. The kept their money in a hole in the ground near their barn.

They lived very simply day to day with plenty of good food and warm clothing-- everything they believed they really needed. They exemplified much of what we of the Smoky Mountains really are--determined, independent, and unpretentious.

Once described as independent as hogs on ice, the Walker Sisters demonstrated a dogged independence while living their primitive life. The six girls who remained in the house never married. When the parents were alive, if young men came calling, they had to leave when Mr. Walker went to bed. That was often shortly after sun down.

Margaret Jane, the oldest daughter, never courted. She apparently decided to become an "Old Maid" early in her life. Through reasoning and ridicule, it appears she attempted to influence the other girls to accept her decision as their own. However, it appears the other girls expected to marry when they were young.

Martha Ann was engaged to John Daniels, who died in an accident. Polly (Mary Elizabeth) was also engaged to marry a logger named Cotter. When he died in an accident, Polly was apparently a student at Carson-Newman College in Jefferson City. Family members reported that when she learned of his death, she walked all night in the rain. Perhaps she attempted to walk the 25-30 miles to her home. Shortly thereafter, she developed an illness with a high fever.

This illness may have affected her mind, because for the rest of her life she was far from the happy person she had once been.

I visited the Walker Sisters at their home near Little Greenbriar Cove in 1947. That they chose to live a very primitive life in no way made our conversation unusual. Our interaction was very much like it would have been in thousands of East Tennessee homes at that time. My family, too, had lived in what is now the Great Smoky Mountain National Park. Our families shared many similar experiences, some of which I will relate to describe life in the Park more fully. My Mother, Mary Jane Ogle Carr Trentham was born close to their home. She was one of their closest neighbors, and, as a young girl, spent many nights with the family. She held these women in such high esteem that I would like to share their story as I have been able to piece it together.

FAMILY HISTORY

Family history is inextricably tied to the history of the region. The story of the Walker family in East Tennessee began in the late 1700's and early 1800's. During that time Scots-Irish and German settlers came from North Carolina and Virginia to live in the Smoky Mountains. Already living in the mountains were settlements of Cherokee Indians. After the Trail of Tears in 1838-39, about 1,000 Cherokees remained in the area. Because Cherokees were required to marry outside their clans, they married more white settlers than most other Native Americans. Many area families can now trace Cherokee ancestry. Because most of the farms were small, few people owned slaves. Consequently, only a small percentage of African-Americans lived in East Tennessee before the Civil War.

Throughout much of the 19th Century, the region remained unchanged except for small family farms, remote coves, and country stores. Most often families walked to stores, schools and churches. Farmers hauled produce to Knoxville over rutted, muddy or dusty unimproved roads. A trip to Knoxville's markets could take as much as three days. The Sevier County census in 1850 showed 1071 heads of families, listing 89 farmers and two who "did nothing." Probably because nearly everyone farmed, many occupations were not listed in this census.

Except for farming, little industry existed in the area. One notable exception was an effort to cut timber in the nearby Elkmont area. One company spent two years building up the waterways to float huge logs down the river. Lumbermen cut some of the most beautiful trees in the area, some as much as 12 feet in diameter. These trees included chestnut, oak, cherry, pine, tulip and yellow poplar. The investors of this company, who invested great sums of money, were from Canada, England, Scotland, and South Africa.

When cloudbursts, as we called them, hit these mountains, the results can be devastating. One of the most discussed cloudbursts hit in 1886, the year of the great flood. Locals called the flood the "Big Britches." Floodwaters carried all the logs and waterways the logging company produced miles and miles down the river. One wag said they went "plumb to the Gulf of Mexico." Local residents stood by shaking their heads at this sight. They were saddened to see all those fine trees cut and left to rot.

After this and other floods bankrupted the company, the principles left the area. The Little River Lumber Company replaced them a few years later. Much of the road through what is now Townsend follows the route of the Little River Lumber Company railroad tracks.

Another underground industry flourished in some mountain hollows ("hollers"), but there is no evidence that it touched the Walker family. A bushel of corn was worth only 20 cents and was very heavy and cumbersome. That same corn made into "Mountain Dew" or moonshine weighed much less and was worth at least $2. Some families distilled the corn and turned an illegal profit.

"Revenuers" in the area searched out and cut down the stills that brewed the liquor. "Moonshiners" sometimes burned barns and gristmills in retaliation. Brawls broke out, and people were sometimes killed. When an otherwise honest, law-abiding citizen, whose children were starving and barefoot, was caught and "lawed," it was hard to find a jury who would convict the moonshiner because jurors understood the circumstances.

Retouched photograph of the John Walker family. Courtesy of Effie Phipps

7

John N. Walker, father of the Walker Sisters was born on March 3, 1841. He was the eldest of 15 children born to Thomas and Eliza Walker. By 1860, John became engaged to Margaret Jane King daughter of Wylie and Mary Jane King. The Civil War delayed the marriage of John and Margaret.

More Civil War battles occurred in Tennessee than in any state except Virginia. Because brothers fought against brothers, fathers fought against sons, and neighbors invariably fought against neighbors, the animosity persisted for decades. The situation in the area was so difficult that some families moved away because of it. In many cases, widows or wives of soldiers remained alone to do the farm work and care for children and farm animals. They had to bury seed corn in the ground to prevent theft by enemy soldiers camped in the area. Of the men who survived to return home, many slept in the woodlands at night to protect themselves and to avoid the plundering, theft, and destruction that continued in and around their homes.

An example of the difficult conditions of local residents involved a Confederate general and a Mrs. Jenkins. The general of the Confederate camp near Sevierville demanded that Mrs. Jenkins cook his breakfast every morning. After some time she complained that because his men had stolen her only mule, she had a very limited supply of food. She could no longer feed the general. He asked if her two children, a boy and girl both under ten years old, would know the mule if they saw it. She said she was sure they would recognize the mule.

The general took the children back to camp, where he showed them mule after mule. They repeatedly shook their heads "no." Finally, an old mule came around the corner of a building. When he saw the children, he "nickered" in recognition. They yelled that this was their mule. The General put them both on the mule and sent them home. He instructed his men never to take anything else from the Jenkins' home.

Despite often dire circumstances, local residents believed lying was sinful. They made a distinction between "white" lies and "black" lies. Even to protect themselves and their families, they were reluctant to lie to enemy soldiers. One family hid a gun in the ground. Rather than tell a "black" lie when asked if they had a gun, a family member replied that they did not have a gun "on the top side of God's Green earth." Technically the statement was true. Similarly, when officers came to seize two men for a crime they were supposed to have committed, family members said the brothers had gone to Green County. The family had named the back bedroom of their home "Green County."

For many the conflict continued long after the Civil War ended. The following oath became common for Confederate sympathizers:

> "Of my own free will and choice, I do hereby in the presence of these witnesses swear to be loyal to the South. When speaking of Yankees, I will refer to them as Scalawags or Carpetbaggers. And I promise to whistle or hum Dixie as a sign of my loyalty and token of my new outlook on life."

One Southern Oath further included a phrase about shooting Yankees "betwixt the galluses" [of their overalls.]

Like the majority of East Tennessee residents, John was a loyal Unionist who held much animosity toward the Confederate cause. In fact, John helped to organize a secret plan to avoid being drafted into the Confederate Army. He and a group of Unionists agreed to steal away, march north, and enlist in the Union Army. The signal for the group to gather and carry out this plan was a bonfire atop Bluff Mountain, a spot so high it was visible for miles around.

According to family tradition, John Walker enlisted in the First Tennessee Light Artillery where he was captured during a battle. He spent approximately 100 days in a Confederate prison. He told his children of poor treatment and starvation, which caused him to lose nearly 100 pounds of weight. During his captivity, a sympathetic farmer dumped a wagonload of pumpkins into the prison compound. This act of kindness eased the hunger pains of the imprisoned Union soldiers. After 100 days, a prisoner exchange took place, which allowed John to go to Cleveland, Ohio where he was discharged. He is not listed in the National Archives, but he drew a small pension.

When John Walker returned to his home at the foot of Cove Mountain in Wears Valley, he found conditions at home very distressing. Confederate soldiers set up a large camp at the site of the former Mountain View Hotel in Gatlinburg, known as Burg Hill. This is now the intersection of highway 321 and 441. When this Confederate camp burned to the ground, this threat to the residents ended.

When the war ended, John resumed his courtship with Margaret Jane, now 20 years old. They married on March 29, 1866. During the next 24 years, Margaret Jane bore eleven babies. James Thomas was the first son. He was born February 22, 1867. Some 19 months later came William Wylie on September 2, 1868. Twenty-three months later on August 29, 1870, Margaret Jane was born and named after her mother. Twenty-six months later came John Henry on Oct. 20, 1872. The last son, Giles Daniel, was born on Oct. 10, 1891. The average size family in the U.S. in 1900 was 5.5; the largest family size was in Tennessee. Whereas large families meant more mouths to feed, children provided help with farm work.

The sisters were Margaret Jane, Mary Elizabeth "Polly," Martha Ann, Louisa Susan, Hettie Rebecca, Nancy Melinda, and Sarah Caroline. Except for Sarah Caroline, who married Jim Shelton, the Walker Sisters remained together on their mountain farm for all but short periods of their lives. Their mother, Margaret Jane King Walker, died on January 15, 1909 after 43 years of marriage. Their father, John, died April 23, 1921.

Margaret Jane chose to be a spinster or old-maid, the terms generally used in those days. Apparently, her efforts to influence her siblings to remain at home had little effect on her brothers, James Thomas, William Wylie, John Henry and Giles Daniel, all of whom married. First-born son, James Thomas, married a daughter of one of the Cole families living near the Chimney Tops. They had three children before her early death. His second wife was "Tip" Stinnett's daughter.

Some time before 1930, the sisters agreed to care for a baby on their farm. Little is know about the child. He was apparently the child of a relative, who was unable to care for him. A family member reported that he was killed around age 21.

According to reports, William Wylie left home about 1910 and settled in Idaho. He was drafted into World War I and fought in numerous engagements, including the Argonne Forest. Giles Daniel "Dan," who deeded his portion of family property to his sisters on Sept. 30, 1921, was the only boy left at home after his brothers moved away. As a young man, Dan married Georgia Moore and divorced soon thereafter. His death on April 18, 1971 made him the last remaining Walker sibling. He was buried in the Maddox Cemetery in Wears Valley, with most of his Walker family.

In addition to their brother, William, at least one nephew fought in the war in Europe. When sending him some socks she knitted, Hettie remarked, "Guess it ain't every soldier in

Germany that can say that his old-maid aunts raised his socks on a rocky mountain-side for him."

The effects of World War I reached even the remote mountain farms. Every boy of draft age was required to have a physical examination even if he was blind or crippled. Draft boards would not accept letters regarding disabilities even from family physicians. During the war, the government asked all citizens to conserve, causing one person to pen the following:

> My Tuesdays are meatless;
> My Wednesdays are wheatless.
> I'm getting less to eat every day.
> My home is heatless;
> My bed is sheetless.
> They are all sent to the YMCA.
>
> The barrooms are treatless;
> My coffee is sweetless.
> Each day I get poorer than dirt.
> My stockings are feetless;
> My trousers are seatless.
> I'm left with only one shirt.

Lasting from 1914 to 1918, World War I significantly changed life in the United States. Farm boys put on uniforms and saw places they had only heard about in geography lessons. When young men of the area returned to their mountain homes, their views of the world were different. It was during this time the line, "How are you going to keep them down on the farm after they've seen Pareee (Paris)?" was penned.

Pressures to open the Great Smoky Mountains National Park began soon thereafter. This decision would forever change the lives of all of us who lived in the Park. It also began the Walker Sisters' struggle to retain their unique way of life.

THEIR HOME

By 1872, with four children under six years old, John began looking for larger quarters and a place of his own. Margaret Jane's parents lived in Little Greenbriar Cove in a split log house they had built. Margaret's siblings had all married and moved away from home. When Margaret's father died in 1859, her mother was left alone. It is reasonable to assume that Mrs. King welcomed John, Margaret, and the four little ones to live with her. Mrs. Wylie King, mother of Mrs. John Walker, lived at the Little Greenbriar home with John and Margaret until her death on June 3, 1886.

By 1877, John and Margaret had six children, the oldest of whom was 10 years old. With Margaret, John, six children, and Margaret's mother, the tiny house was most certainly crowded. John dismantled an old log cabin nearby and used the material to build a kitchen addition to the home. He also added the front porch at that time. After that addition, only minor changes and repairs were made to the house. The family replaced the roof from time to time, and the floor, currently found in the house, was replaced only once. Periodic replacement of the mud, which chinked the six-foot fireplace, was required to endure cold and sometimes isolated winters.

Although Margaret's brothers and sisters appeared to raise no objection when the Walker family moved in with Margaret's mother, some family members attempted to block his ownership of the property. Initially John was able to purchase the interest of the family's home from five of the heirs. Four of the heirs, however, refused to sell. With all the improvements to the house, it appeared to the siblings that John "was sitting too high on the hog." They insisted that he should pay them rent. John refused to pay. A distant relative, Betty A. King, managed to acquire two of the remaining four one-tenths shares not owned by Walker. She filed suit in court regarding the matter. The court ruling placed the four remaining shares in public auction. With a high bid of $300 John became the sole owner on April 23, 1893.

John was known as Hairy John because he grew a long beard to distinguish himself from all the other John Walkers in the area. He was a very talented man. He built the additions to the house and all the outbuildings. He constructed a barn, pigpen, corncrib, blacksmith shop, smokehouse, apple house, gristmill, and springhouse. In addition to the poultry yard, there was an ash hopper, a tar kiln, a drying rack, and a charcoal-making pit. To enclose the garden, he also built the paling fences. These were made of four-inch-wide-boards about thirty-six inches long with wire crossed between each board.

John Walker built every building the family needed except for an "outhouse." The women used the woodland below the house; the men used the woodland above the house. No outhouse ever sat on the property. Officials of the Works Progress Administration (WPA) and others offered to construct such a unit, but the Walker Sisters always refused. Margaret, the oldest daughter, known as the Boss-Cook refused to allow an outhouse on the property. She said that an outhouse would smell and that having people know what it was used for would embarrass the sisters.

Methods of construction were very different than today. Farmers used whole logs or logs split down the center to construct most buildings. Door hinges such as those on the springhouse were called pintles or gudgeons. A gudgeon was a round pole the length of the door. This pole pivoted on each end and was set in a recessed hole in which it could turn. A board at the top and bottom held the pole in place. When the door opened or closed, it pivoted in the hole.

The Walker Sisters' home as it looks today. Courtesy of Effie Phipps.

Horseshoes attached to the kitchen windows functioned as hinges. If a windowpane was broken, they smeared a heavy coarse paper with bear grease and placed it over the glass until they could find a proper replacement. The bear grease made the paper somewhat transparent.

Hairy John was a carpenter, handyman, farmer, sheep and goat herder, doctor, dentist, and veterinarian. He constructed the family's furniture and looms as well as their five spinning wheels. It would be virtually impossible to describe the interior of the Walker Sisters' house. The house was always clean as a pin. Not a speck of dirt was on the floors. However, someone who saw it used the term "organized confusion."

The living room served as the bedroom for the parents and all the girls. The boys slept in the attic or loft, where there were more beds, chairs, and chests with many items attached to the walls and ceiling. To reach the upper bedroom or loft one had to climb a ladder attached to the wall.

The five three-quarter sized beds downstairs and a trundle bed provided places for everyone to sleep. The furniture included a table with chairs and two dressers. Five spinning wheels and several chairs were also in this room. Life became somewhat easier when the family acquired two wood-burning cook-stoves and a sewing machine. The house also contained all the family's clothing, linens, and other household goods such as kerosene lamps and cooking equipment.

On the dressers were many tintype pictures of the family. The girls used newspapers, magazines, calendars, letters, family pictures, religious scenes, and greeting cards that struck their fancy as "wallpaper" for the walls. In addition to the wall decorations, many other items hung on nails around the house. These included clocks, dried foods, clothing, yarn, thread, guns, crutches, kitchen utensils, magazines, baskets, spice racks, lanterns, and bags of seeds. Every year the Walker Sisters moved all the furniture outside to scour all the walls with boiling water. After they replaced the "wallpaper," they returned everything to its usual place. First, they replaced the furniture. Then they replaced the hundreds of items that hung on the walls.

An incredible variety of items covered the wall space-- even to the rafters upstairs. Until the barn was built, saddles dangled from nails in the living room. In the loft, large shoeboxes and other much larger items hung on the walls. These were not visible from the living room/bedroom downstairs. Amazingly, everyone seemed to know exactly where to find every item.

Baskets from the Walker home. Courtesy of Great Smoky Mountains National Park Museum Collection, Gatlinburg, Tennessee.

In the back of the large fireplace was a back-stick, a large log used to force the burning logs toward the front to reflect heat into the room. This back-stick burned and required replacement about once a week. If any of the previous back-stick remained, they pulled it to the front and placed it on the dog irons to give room for the new back-stick.

Their old mule pulled the new log to the door. Placing round poles on the cabin floor helped them to roll the enormous log to the fireplace. A peavey, a handheld rod about five feet long, helped to place the log. The peavey had a moveable hook fastened about eighteen inches from the bottom that allowed them to pry or move heavy objects, especially logs.

Placing the back-stick was too strenuous for the Sisters. When their father and brothers were no longer available, neighbors came to install their back-sticks. Fred Walker, a 90-year-old nephew, living in Wears Valley, said he and others performed this chore for them once a week. Friends and devoted nieces and nephews spent as much as three days a week helping with different farm chores.

In the floor in front of the fireplace was an underground trap door exposing a cellar where they stored Irish potatoes for the winter. The crowded kitchen contained a large table with benches, chairs, two cook stoves, a worktable, water shelf, jelly box, salt gum, loom, cupboard, and meal and flour bins made from hollow gum logs.

The kitchen also contained a fireplace with a trap door located in front of it. The family stored sweet potatoes in this cellar. When the floor was replaced, they eliminated the trap doors. There was also a storage space over the kitchen, which held hundreds of items. When someone asked one of the sisters what was in that space, she replied, "Lord, everything!" They saved every item that might later be of any use. The Walker Sisters firmly believed in the old adage "Waste not; want not."

The sisters purchased a hand-held gristmill to grind corn for their cornbread rather than to carry it to a water-powered mill. This gristmill ground corn for Kit, their old mule with bad teeth. This mule grew so cantankerous or "mule-headed" in his old days that the sisters could not use him to plow the garden or drag in firewood. They asked a relative to help them with the mule saying that "a 'Tennessee Mule' had to be handled special, because none of them could cuss!"

The grounds around the house displayed the beauties of nature. The sisters tended over 100 varieties of flowers and shrubs. Their flowers included snowballs, lilacs, hydrangeas, and more than thirty varieties of roses. Rock piles arranged in and around the flowers added to the beauty of their home.

Walker Sisters' living room with unidentified woman.

Louisa was said to be the feistiest of the girls. She made much sport of all the bachelor button flowers that grew among the other flowers. She said, as old maids, they could keep hoping. They called their flowers "pretties" or "Easter flowers." The irises were called flags, while peonies were called pinnies. There was no grass in the yard. The sisters swept it clean with a large homemade broom.

Not all the surroundings were enjoyable, however. One avoided the Spanish needles, cockleburs, beggar lice and chiggers (sometimes called redbugs.) The first three stick to clothing and are difficult to remove. Chiggers penetrated the skin and itched unmercifully.

The long-empty house visitors see today is as it appeared in the 1870's.

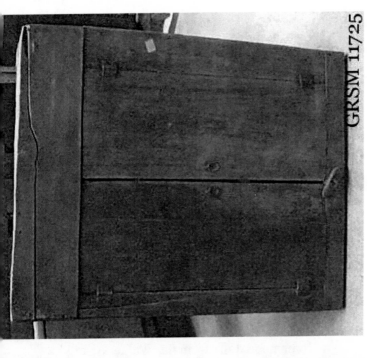

Chests from the Walker Sisters' home. Courtesy of Great Smoky Mountains National Park Museum Collection, Gatlinburg, Tennessee.

21

Homemade dolls from the Walker Sisters'
Home. Courtesy of Great Smoky Mountains
National Park Museum Collection,
Gatlinburg. Tennessee.

FAMILY LIFE

John Walker was very devoted to his family. Every year when the crops were "laid by" he took the boys on a two-week camping trip to fish and hunt. He was, however, very stern. His overly strict manner could have been one reason some of his children chose not to marry. He usually went to bed with the chickens (when it was dark) and he expected the girls to do likewise. My mother said when she spent the night at their home, Mr. Walker got out of bed very early and would call to the girls, saying "Pol, Het, Marg, Lou, Nance, get up!" The girls quickly obeyed. The sisters considered Margaret Jane, the oldest daughter, the boss. It was the norm at that time for the oldest daughter to have authority over all the younger children.

Their mother, a typical mountain woman, bore 11 children at home in a 24-year period. Each one reached maturity. She had none of the modern conveniences for babies. All diapers were cloth, probably made from torn bed sheets. Mothers boiled diapers in a large black pot after each use. Parents made teething rings from pieces of pork rind. They tied one end of a string to the pork rind and the other to the baby's big toe. If the baby started to choke on the rind, he would kick his feet and legs, which would pull the rind out of his mouth. Baby food was also very different than today. Families had no blenders, and no baby food was available in stores. As unsanitary as it sounds, mothers chewed the food for babies and then put it into their mouths.

Babies of both sexes wore dresses until they were four or five years old. When the mother attended to chores outside, it was unsafe to leave a toddler alone or with other young children. When the toddler wore a long dress, the mother could lift the bed leg, set it on the dress tail, and know the baby would at least stay in one place.

Their daily lives were filled with work like few know today. It is possible that Margaret put pressure on the other girls not to marry because of the overwhelming load of chores required to maintain their lives. One less worker would have made a great difference in the workload.

It is hard to imagine all the work involved in making clothing and shoes while growing all the food and carving all the furniture. One wonders how they could do all the work required to take care of their needs. Maybe getting up at 3:00 or 4:00 a.m. helps to account for that. The family had well-planned schedules with each person knowing exactly which chore was hers.

All their lives the girls wore homemade ankle-length, long-sleeved dresses and bonnets when outside. During that time, women tried to avoid any touch of suntan. Apparently, because it indicated women did not have to work in the fields, women considered very white skin desirable.

On their feet the sisters wore homemade high-top beef hide shoes along with handmade socks or stockings. They tanned squirrel hides for shoestrings or "shoe laces." A "peggin' awl," which looked like a short ice pick, was used to make holes in the shoes. They greased boots and shoes with sheep or beef tallow (taller) particularly around the holes made by the peggin' awl.

The sisters always wore bonnets and heavy shoes to church. Everyone called clothing worn to church "Sunday-go-to-meetin'" clothes." Some women in the area simply took off their aprons, turned them inside out, and "presto" they were ready to go. (I have seen women do this.) We do not know if the Walker women ever dressed for church this way.

In winter, the sisters wore heavy home-woven linsey-woolsey dresses and coats. They grew cotton and flax for underclothing, linens, dresses, etc. Material for cooler summer clothing was sometimes "store-bought." The pattern for all the dresses appeared to be the same one. The family considered Nancy to be a great needlepoint woman who could make near-perfect buttonholes. Perhaps their married sister Caroline wore more modern clothing.

Spinning wheel from the Walkers' home. Courtesy of Great Smoky Mountains National Park Museum Collection, Gatlinburg, Tennessee.

Waking up in a cold house was never enjoyable, and remaining warm during the cold winters was a challenge. Long underwear was a big help. When it became cold, male family members wore "long-johns" under their clothing. The "long-johns" had to have a slit in the front and "trap-door" in the back. Women wore additional knitted or crocheted underwear.

Making their clothing, underclothing, shoes, socks, stockings, linens, and bed clothing was extremely time-consuming. They even made saddle blankets for their mules, Beck and Kit. Every one of the girls could hogtie bleating and kicking sheep to shear for wool. That was only the first step in making the heavy linsey-woolsey fabric they wore. They also had to gather barks to dye the different colored wools they wove.

They washed, dried, corded, and spun cotton, flax, and wool into thread. For many years, five spinning wheels ran in the house at the same time. Looms were also there to weave the thread into cloth. Then they had to sew all the pieces together.

Many tourists came repeatedly to see them perform these and many other household chores. While cooking or doing other work, they rolled up the long sleeves of their dresses. If one of the sisters saw a visitor coming, she would always roll down her sleeves.

Because there were no barbershops or hairdressers, the mother or sisters cut hair for their father and brothers. However, they reserved the time between the full moon and the last quarter of the moon to cut hair, because they believed hair grew more slowly if cut during that time. A few people still swear by that method.

Even until the late 1930's mountain women wore long hair. It was usually gathered and wrapped around their heads in buns. According to the preachers, a woman's hair was her "Glory." My Mother-in-law, Ida Headrick Myers, cut her hair as the trend for long hair began to change. There was discussion about "turning her out" of her church in Wears Valley. My two older sisters had to wear long hair. I do not know how I escaped. My hair was never long.

The sisters had only homemade soap and vinegar for shampoo. No feminine hygiene products were available. During their monthly periods, they added petticoats to absorb the flow.

During the summer, tree leaves or corncobs usually served as toilet tissue. There were both white and red corncobs. The joke

26

was that you used a red corncob first. Then you used a white cob to see if you needed to use another red cob. The cobs were pretty rough. In winter when no leaves were available, strips of newspaper or washable rags served this purpose. My late husband, Ray T. Myers, claimed he once mistakenly used poison ivy leaves for this purpose.

Goose quills functioned as toothpicks. Straw tick mattresses were made of cornshucks. These were filled anew each fall after the harvest. Egg whites or a paste of flour and water served as glue. When traveling by buggy, wagon, or sled in the winter, heated rocks or hot coals from the fireplace were wrapped and put at the feet. I remember watching my father put huge flat rocks in the fireplace at night. When the rocks were hot, he wrapped them well in newspapers and then in burlap or cotton sacks. Travelers placed their cold feet on the rocks and then covered with woolen lap robes for a small amount of warmth.

When the weather became cold around the first frost, mountain people would comment that it was hog-killing time. Hog killing took place only when the signs (moon and zodiac) were right and the water was boiling hot. Generally, they used a gun or sledgehammer to kill the hogs. Afterwards, a long knife was inserted into the large artery near the heart to drain the blood. After scalding the hog, they hung it by the rear feet to scrape the hairs. Then they split it down the middle underneath to remove the entrails.

The animal was cut into sections: shoulders, hams, backbone, etc. After this was finished, much work remained. The sausage and tenderloins were canned; hams and shoulders were smoked or salted down; and, the head was used to produce souse meat. After cleaning the hog's head, they boiled it until tender. Once cooled, they separated the meat from the bones. After adding salt, sage, and pepper, they formed the souse into a loaf. The loaf kept for about a week.

After salting down some of the side and shoulder meat for a few weeks, they cleansed and smoked it. Brown sugar, pepper, salt, and honey or molasses were added for a very flavorful smoked ham. They fried or cooked salt-cured ham in dried beans.

If ham meat was too salty, they boiled it in water to remove some of the salt. Then it was fried in an iron skillet with lard. They made red-eye gravy from the residue. After removing the meat, they added coffee and water to the skillet drippings. After boiling the mixture, they poured the gravy over bread or potatoes. It was not thick like flour gravy, but it was very tasty. Cornmeal gravy was also popular. When it is well seasoned, it tastes great.

They used the hog's urinary bladder to make a kickball or basketball. After cleaning it, they blew it up and tied it into a balloon. When placed in a fire, the ball exploded like the sound of a shotgun.

Activities that required a number of family members lent themselves to story telling. The local story that always went with hog-killing time in our area was a true story originating with one of the Ogle families I knew. The boys acquired a book of instructions telling step-by-step how to slaughter a hog. Instructions in the book were very much contrary to what their father had done very successfully for many years. In fact, when it came time to hang the hog to scrape the hair and cut it, a real disagreement arose. The sons, who quoted the instructions, ignored the father's insistent comments that the book was wrong. As the father predicted, the hog fell into the mess below. The father could not resist asking, "Well, boys, what does the book say about that?"

The family used fat from slaughtered hogs to make their lye soap. First they cut the fat away from the lean meat. They put the fat aside until time to make the soap, usually right away. Throughout the year, until hog-killing time, the family carefully collected ashes from the cook stove and inside fireplace to put into an "ash hopper." When ready to make soap, they poured water over the ashes several times and caught the liquid in a container. This product, a strong alkali, was commonly called "lye."

To make the soap, they heated the fat outside over a fire in a thoroughly cleaned, large black wash kettle. When all the fat cooked out, they strained the cracklings (sold in stores today) and retained them for cooking. They combined the lye mixture from the ashes with the fat as it cooked over the fire. Someone had to stir this mixture with a sassafras paddle every minute.

When the mixture appeared to have reached the proper consistency, they dipped a chicken, duck or goose feather into the soap-making mixture. If the lye was too strong it ate away the soft bristle, leaving only the quill or bony part of the feather. This meant more fat was required. When the mixture was finally ready, they poured it onto boards or pans or left it in the wash pot to cool overnight. Once it cooled and hardened, they cut the soap into cubes about three inches long and perhaps two inches wide, much like large bars of soap today.

The cut soap was used for bathing, washing, and general cleaning. When vanilla became available in local stores, they added it to part of the soap mixture before it hardened. They called this "special soap" and used it only for bathing. They used plain soap for cleaning, dishwashing and laundry. Some soap was placed in containers with water to make liquid soap.

Bathing was a complicated affair. During the week, family members bathed using a pail of water and a washcloth. In the area it was the practice for everyone to bathe on Saturday night (whether he needed it or not.) My family enjoyed the often-told story of the mountain girl who took a job with a family in the city. This family had a nice bathtub. She wrote her family that she could hardly wait until Saturday night so she could take a bath in the tub.

It is reasonable to assume that the Walker family took tub baths and changed their clothing on Saturday night as well. It appears that they used wooden rather than galvanized tubs. Family members could take turns bathing in a large tub usually placed behind the kitchen stove. They heated water on the stove and poured it into the tub. (I remember that well.) They had to carry all water from the spring to the kitchen. For that reason, it is unlikely that all members of the family had fresh bath water.

After their Saturday-night baths, they wore their best dresses to church on Sunday. Monday was washday throughout the region. Washday found clothes boiling in a big black iron wash pot in the yard. They used a "battling stick," a pole about four feet long, to move the clothing around in the wash pot. They poured bluing in the rinse water to brighten their white clothes. After wringing out the water by hand, they hung the clothes over a clothesline or over the paling fence to dry in the sun. They had only wooden clothespins back then. These were pieces of wood about five inches long and split up the middle.

We are not sure which method the Walkers used to iron their clothing. Some people used flat irons which were placed before the hot fire in the fireplace. To prevent smudging the clothing, one had to be careful to remove all ashes which might cling to the iron. Those who did not use flat irons simply folded the articles and put them in a chairs or under a mattresses to smooth them out.

They had to use much "elbow grease" to keep their house "eat-off-the floor" clean. They reused wash water to clean the floors in the house. The long-handled homemade mop was a wide board with several holes bored through it. Cornhusks or shucks were pulled through the holes to make the mop head.

Although galvanized products became available in rural stores and from traveling salesmen about the time the girls were born, many of the vessels the Walker Sisters used were hewn-out logs. In fact, the sisters were still using their wooden buckets and gourd dippers for guests in their final years.

They used wood for bowls and plates. Even the dough board was flat wood hollowed out on the top side. They also made wooden buckets and washtubs in which wire held the wood pieces together. The wood used to make tubs or buckets held enough water to make the wood swell. This prevented the container from leaking.

Until they purchased the wood-burning cook stoves, they used iron Dutch ovens which hung over the open fire. Potatoes and onions were placed in the hot ashes for baking. Until about 1890 when matches became available, the family kept a fire burning in the fireplace at all times. The Walkers' fireplace was 6 feet wide. They "banked" the fire at bedtime, meaning they covered the hot coals with lots of ashes. When uncovered the next morning, a roaring fire soon flamed as rich pine kindling was added.

In the evening, the family sat in the dark, lit an oil lamp, or went to bed early. When they sat outside in the yard, gnats were likely to bite them. A "gnat smoke" would have provided them with some protection. To make a gnat smoke, they placed cotton rags on top of coals of fire in a small container. The rags smoldered, which provided smoke to drive away the gnats.

Mountain families, including the Walker Sisters, rarely refused a guest's request to spend the night. Some families, however, lived in one-room cabins. A stranger who was taken in was directed to the bed where he could sleep. Often, the guest slept with his clothes on. In homes with large families, a visitor might find himself in bed with three or more children.

When company came, the Walker Sisters pulled out the trundle bed and allowed their guests "to sleep the sleep of the just." My mother mentioned sleeping on the trundle bed while spending the night at their home. At bedtime, the father went to bed first. Everyone in the room turned their faces in the opposite direction. Then they blew out the lighted oil lamp to allow the women folk to undress and change into nightwear.

If a family member or their guests found it necessary to answer nature's call during the night, he or she used a yellow (yaller) "thunder mug." Since families did not have indoor plumbing, a thunder mug was a necessity. Who in his right mind is going outside in the dark, where he might step on or squat on a rattlesnake or copperhead?

MEALTIME

The family ate three meals a day- breakfast, dinner and supper. No one in the area used the term "lunch" to describe the noon meal. They cooked all their meals at the six-foot wide fireplace until two cook stoves became available for the kitchen. Family meals were elaborate and of greater variety than was found in most early homes. With all the food preservation and other chores, one wonders how these women had time to prepare such sumptuous meals.

Before each meal the food was "blessed." Margaret often took care of that duty. Her prayers were very long as she told her deceased mother about their lives. She mentioned most of the chores including the progress of all the crops in the fields and gardens. She discussed what she felt would be most pleasing about how well things were progressing during her mother's absence.

The breakfast menu was always the same... hot coffee, cat-head biscuits (very large) made from scratch, saw-mill gravy, eggs and sausage, bacon, or ham. Then they spread butter and jelly or preserves on the biscuits. Before coffee became available in their store, they boiled dandelion roots or chestnuts to drink. These were dried and parched on the stove and then ground in a mill that hung on the kitchen wall. After their noon meal (dinner), they covered food items with a clean sheet or tablecloth, and the food remained on the table for supper.

Many meals included cornbread baked in a Dutch oven. It was served hot and smothered with fresh-churned butter. In the days before germs and vitamins were recognized, some people licked the knife before cutting into the butter.

Bread required baking soda (introduced just after the Civil War) and baking powder (which became available around 1895.) There was no self-rising flour or cornmeal then. Before these products became available, ash hoppers were probably the only source of anything akin to soda or baking powder.

Some say the family mainly ate mutton, but others say venison with cherry sauce was a favorite dish. Chicken was often on the menu. They ate little beef, because it was tough and bluish in color due to the diet of the cattle. The family raised many sheep during the early days, but later wild dogs killed so many sheep they kept only a few. When the sisters' last cow died, they never purchased another. They preferred to use the milk from their goats.

Huge five-gallon crocks held milk, butter, sauerkraut, pickled beets, cucumbers and pickled okra. They placed all these in the springhouse to keep them cool. Milk and butter usually sat directly in the cold water of the springhouse.

It was necessary to churn milk to make butter. This required pouring the milk into a churn jar. Then they spent many hours moving a "churn dash" up and down in the jar until butter eventually separated from the milk. During the winter, it was necessary to turn the churn jar around in front of the fire so it would be the right "kelter" for churning. Unless the temperature was correct, the milk would not "clabber" or become thick by souring. It was the clabbering, which created the butter.

Although home canning became possible after 1858, it would have been difficult for the sisters to use many home canning products on their wood cook stoves. However, in later years they may have preserved some of their food using mason jars. Preserved food was also dried, pickled, sulphured, or salted. They stored salted meats on a board in the springhouse. Storekeepers sold salt in 100-pound bags. The family stored the salt in a hollow gum in the kitchen. Earlier salt came in crystal blocks. They kept it in a saltcellar somewhere under a building to keep it dry and accessible. They chipped salt from this block for cooking and seasoning.

Root crops like potatoes were stored in the apple house or in the cellars under the floor. They cut pumpkins into small strips and dried them on racks near the fireplace. They dried apples, peaches, plums, pumpkins, and beans and placed them in cloth containers. Then they hung the dried food on nails somewhere in the house.

Houseflies were a real problem for the Walker family before the introduction of screen wire. To stay cool in summer, doors and windows remained open. Of course, flies gathered around the dinner table. A "fly-sweep" was made of thin strips of newspaper fastened to a pole and mounted on a contraption that sat on the floor under the table. While he was still living, Mr. Walker kept his foot on the pedal of the contraption to shoo flies away from the food. Sometimes the contraption broke down and the rope that pulled newspapers back and forth across the table was fastened to a nail driven in the corner of the table.

One of my friends described a meal she ate at the Walker Sisters' home when the fly sweep was broken. She was a young child and remembered becoming bored after what seemed like fifteen minutes of Margaret's blessing of the food. During the prayer, my friend pulled the rope tied to the nail in the corner of the dining table. This activity moved the fly sweep's newspapers back and forth over the table creating a slight noise. She remembers being "shushed" for being irreverent. She was told to act "pert."

Although mountain farms are not overly productive, the Walkers seemed to have the necessities. Their table usually provided a bountiful feast. Special meals were prepared for Christmas and other special occasions. Margaret started preparing specialties several days before Christmas. Stack cakes were very high on the list. Few cooks wrote their recipes at that time. Recipes consisted of a pinch of this or a dab of that. The following would closely approximate a stack cake recipe, which varied depending upon the number of layers or desired height.

STACK CAKE RECIPE
In three or more cups of water, cook about ten cups of dried apples until tender.

APPLESAUCE MIXTURE
Drain the applesauce if it is too thin.
Add 1/3 cup sugar for each cup of apples.
Add cinnamon, nutmeg and vanilla to taste.

STACKING CAKES MIXTURE
4 ½ cups flour
1 ½ cup shortening (Hogs lard, then)
1 ½ tsp soda for that much flour
3/4 tsp salt
Mix well and combine the following:
3 beaten eggs
1 ½ cup sugar
4 ½ tbsp cream
1 ½ tsp vanilla

Combine both mixtures. Bake in thin layers, maybe 4 or 6 layers depending on the size pan or height of cake.

FARMING

The Walker Sisters used their 122.8 acres of land as best they could. Living off the land required great ingenuity and extremely hard work. They could use guns or dogs to protect themselves from nearly everything but forest fires. The sisters spent their lives digging in the earth with a mattock, planting, and cultivating all the food they ate. They seemed to enjoy every minute of it. People who knew them reported that they regularly sang old hymns while they worked.

Hairy John made their wooden plows. No doubt, the Walker family may also have used metal plow points. When the first metal plows became available in the mountains in the 1830's, the people were afraid that they might poison the soil. It sounds funny to us today, but during those days anything unknown was questioned and often feared. The same thing occurred when electricity first became available. Some people were afraid to eat cornbread baked in an early electric oven.

In the very early days, the family paid cash only for salt and nails. As time went on bolt cloth, horseshoes, coffee, tobacco, cigarette papers, stick candy, castor oil, Epsom salts, baking soda, baking powder, cheese, soda crackers, pork and beans, sewing thread, needles, kerosene, axle grease, slates, pencils and writing tablets became available. They bought or bartered for items from the General Store or their neighbors.

They used the honey from their bees as a sweetener. They could also use maple sugar from the Sugarlands. Until the Park was created, residents of the area enjoyed the syrup and sugar the maple trees there provided.

Around 1920 Octagon and Ivory soap and ground coffee in bulk became available. For some idea of cost, in a general store in 1910, milk sold for 20 cents per gallon, buttermilk was 10 cents.

The cost of butter was 15 cents per pound. Blackberries were ten cents per gallon. One egg bought a full bag of candy.

After tourists began to come to their home, they took in money selling products such as ginseng, possum grapes, hickory nuts, molasses, honey, woven place mats, towels, doilies and coverlets. With the additional income, they added additional items to the list of purchases. They no longer had to make substitutes for coffee, sugar, or baking soda.

To prepare the ground for planting, they burned the brush to clear the land as well as to enrich the soil with ashes. Commercial fertilizers were not generally available in the U.S. until the 1920's. As their use grew, it is likely the Walker Sisters began to purchase fertilizers for their crops. However, farmers commonly saved chicken droppings and manure from the barn lot for this use. Some gardeners still use cow and horse dropping around tomatoes and other vegetables.

The family laid out their garden behind the house and built a paling fence around it. Farther from the house, they cleared fields for larger crops such as wheat and potatoes. They grew both Irish and sweet potatoes behind the apple house. Above the main house was the great blue Concord grape arbor. Wine or other strong drinks generally were forbidden in the Walker household. However, people said that Smoky Mountain wine would awaken the dead and delight the angels.

The vegetables grown on the farm consisted of corn, okra, cabbage, green beans, radishes, lettuce, onions, beans, peas, tomatoes, and both sweet and Irish potatoes. Along with the orchards for apples, peaches, plums and cherries were chestnuts and many other less important crops such as tobacco to chew, smoke or dip as snuff.

The apple orchard contained more than twenty varieties of apples. These included names such as Ben Davis, Rambo, Limber-twig, Red Milam, Red June, Sour John, Abraham, Shockley, Buckingham and others. All the different varieties ripened at different times of the year giving the family a steady diet of apples and reducing spoilage that would occur if all the fruit ripened at the same time.

Fred Walker, a nephew, said they had over 100 apple trees and every meal included applesauce, apple jelly, apple butter, apple pies or apple dumplings. They also made apple cider vinegar, which has many household cooking and cleaning uses. Residents in the area used vinegar to treat many illnesses or conditions. These include asthma, stomach ailments, high blood pressure, insect bites, burns, sore throats, sunburns, coughs, and hiccups. Some said vinegar would fade age spots and treat cancer.

The family also dried apples to preserve them. First, they peeled them and cut them into small slices. So air could easily circulate, they placed apple pieces on screens they removed from their windows. This allowed the apples to dry more quickly. To speed the drying process, they dried other apples on the roof of the outbuildings. It took ten bushels of fresh apples to make one bushel of dried fruit.

The family took great care to preserve foods. Until canning jars became available, apples were dried or sulphured. Sulphured apples were produced by placing peeled and quartered apples in a dry kiln in which sulphur was burned. When the apples dried, they were packed in five-gallon jars. This preservative made a very flavorful and enjoyable apple dish. My mother always had a large crock of sulphured apples. When they were cooked, one did not detect the sulphur taste--just fresh-tasting apples.

They enjoyed eating "crapped cabbage" in the early spring as they looked forward to some fresh vegetables. They stripped the large lower leaves of the cabbage plant and cooked them in water. Removing those leaves did not affect the growth of the forming cabbage head. After harvesting cabbage, they stored it below the frost line for the winter. Storing cabbage under ground required digging a hole in sloping ground so that rainwater could easily drain away. The hole was lined with straw and covered with more straw and dirt. When they wanted cabbage during the winter, they uncovered and removed the cabbage heads.

Dried beans were called "shab" or fodder beans. They were dried in the sun, put in a cloth sack, and hung on a wall inside the house. October beans remained in the field to dry. Then they were picked and placed between two sheets. Family members used a flailing pole to beat the beans. This caused the hulls to fall off. When they lifted the sheets, the wind blew the chaff away, leaving the beans intact. These sold for $4 or $5 per bushel.

Then there were all the nuts: chestnuts, hickory nuts, walnuts, hazelnuts, and other smaller ones. When there was a surplus of nuts, they were used as cash crops or for bartering along with surplus apples, grapes and especially ginseng. Wild berries grew around the farm as well. They gathered these during the summer. Berry picking invariably subjected the picker to insect bites. To avoid chigger bites, they used pennyroyal to rub on wrists and ankles. To relieve the itch of insect bites, they mixed baking soda with a small amount of water and applied the mixture to the bite.

Growing broomcorn and tying the brooms required skill. A broomcorn plant looks much like a corn stalk. It has leaf-like shoots that grow out of the top and sides along with spikes 18 to 24 inches long. At the end of each of these spikes are many straws covered with seeds. The spike is perhaps the size of one's middle finger and has a solid bark or covering about two-thirds the length of it. One took a dull knife or knife back and pushed the seeds off the straws. They reserved the seeds for the next crop. Many spikes were bound to the broom handle by wire, heavy string, or twine. A nail fastened the spikes to the end of the broom handle. The straws were then trimmed flat at the end to make the broom ready to sweep the floor.

Ramps (rampions), a member of the onion family, grew wild in the area. Mountain people loved their sweet taste. However, body odor could remain for one to two weeks after eating just one ramp. One's only defense against the odor was to eat ramps also. Teachers sent youngsters home from school if they had eaten ramps, because the odor of just one child, who had eaten ramps, could pollute an entire schoolroom.

Some of the fields were on steep hillsides. Hoeing corn on hills such as these would require family members to move along on their knees. When digging crops, mountain farmers could count on potatoes to roll to the bottom of the hill when they were unearthed. On very steep hills, sometimes a rock would be propped against a stalk of corn to make it stand up. After hillsides were cleared of trees the rain could wash away much of the rich top soil. When that happened, locals said a hill farmer was as poor as Job's turkey-- too poor to gobble.

Hillside farming presented a common problem in the area. One of the cornfields at our home in the Park was extremely steep-determined to have a 50-degree angle. While hoeing on this particular hillside, my Dad told my sister, "You can't hoe corn with your rump up the hill!" I will never forget the day a traveling salesman climbed way up toward the top of that hill and said to us, "Anyone who would hoe corn on this hill will steal." My Mother was ready to flog him good when he qualified that statement by saying, "because you have to steal dirt from another place to dress the corn." Traveling salesmen wanted to get your attention.

Crows were another problem. I believe every farmer had trouble with crows taking up very young corn plants. When new corn plants were three to five inches high, the grain of corn remained on the root. Crows pulled up the plant and ate the grain of corn. The plant, of course, died. The damage a large flock of crows could do in just one day was amazing.

Many farmers made elaborate scarecrows (we called them "scarcrows") and placed them in the cornfields. They usually built a wood frame with a crosspiece near the top. Then they stuffed a pair of overalls with straw or other sturdy material and attached it to the middle of the post. They put a shirt on the "arms" of the crosspiece. They stuffed cloth or other material to make a head and neck. They placed this on the top of the post. When they put an old straw hat on the head, it appeared that a person was in the field. Scarecrows helped a little.

The only way found to stop crows was to kill one crow and hang it on a pole in the garden. When the entire covey of crows arrived the next day, they saw their companion and made noises like those that few have ever heard. They mourn in different pitches for about thirty minutes as they gather close around the pole where the dead bird hangs. They do not bother the corn crop again. However, to be able to kill a crow is virtually impossible.

Signs of the Zodiac determined when to do all planting. Each year farmers obtained "Farmers' Almanacs" or calendars showing the moon signs associated with the constellations of the Zodiac. Special symbols told in which constellation the moon could be found during its 28-day cycle. Beliefs regarding planting that were common in the area include the following:

-Always plant wheat during the full moon.
-Always plant a garden on the 100th day of the year or on
      Good Friday if possible.
-To have plenty of beans, plant when the sign is in the arms.
-Cabbage seed must be sewn when the sign is in the head.

-Plant and dig potatoes when the sign is in the heart.

-Plant beets when the sign is in the heart.

-Never plant anything but flowers when the sign is in the bowels. Plants produce only blossoms.

-Plant corn on the dark of the moon, or it will grow too tall.

-Plant okra, beans, and corn early in the morning and during the old moon.

-If a farmer plants corn when he is mad, the corn will all be smut (a black powder mold that forms on the ear of corn, which makes it inedible.)

-To kill a tree they waited until the sign was in the heart. Then they cut a deep ring around the tree to kill it.

-If the sign were in the bowels or privates, sometimes called the flowers, potatoes would bloom with great profusion, but not make potatoes.

-Set posts in the ground on the dark nights of the moon and they act as if they grew there.

-Barnyard manure lies on top of the ground for 3 to 5 years if it is spread during the full moon.

I was very skeptical about moon signs, but two experiences made me wonder. When I scoffed about some of the beliefs, my father, Noah Trentham, demonstrated how objects sank or stayed on top of the ground depending upon when they were placed there. He placed two boards on the ground: one during the full moon and the other when the moon was barely visible. The boards placed during the full moon curled up on each end and would not settle into the ground. The boards placed during dark nights went right into the ground and made a good walkway.

My husband and I planted some potatoes when, according to the almanac, the moon was in the bowels. My father-in-law, W. Bruce Myers, told us we would not "get our seed back." Because the plants were so beautiful and lush, we were convinced he was wrong. When it came time to dig the potatoes, we discovered there was practically nothing under those beautiful plants.

43

Beliefs in moon signs and other superstitious ideas were common because life could be so tenuous. Too little or too much rain, a drought, or late frost could ruin the crops. Farmers relied on everything they could to insure good harvests. An old saying describing that concern was, "Old Adam was a gardener, and God who made him see, that half a proper gardener's work is done upon his knees."

FARM ANIMALS

Considering all the hard work required to feed, water, care for injured or sick animals, and protect themselves and their animals from danger, it is little wonder the family had to get out of bed at 3:00 or 4:00 a.m. Milking was a daily chore. The food they produced on the farm had to feed the animals as well as the family, particularly during the winter months. Food for the oxen, mules or cows consisted of dried hay from the fields, shelled corn, or blades pulled off the corn stalks. Shelled corn was the chief food for the chickens.

Most of their lives the sisters kept a couple of cows for milk and butter. They kept chickens for eggs and meat for the table, pork for ham, bacon and sausage, sheep for mutton and wool, goats for milk and meat, as well as bees for honey. Wild turkeys, deer, possums, groundhogs, rabbits, squirrels, bears and wild boars were also available.

Most mountain families raised the Rhode Island Red and Dominecker chickens. When they became available, the Walker Sisters raised Red Indian game chickens, a rare breed of long-necked, black chickens whose drumsticks were smaller than the average chicken. When asked why they chose these chickens rather than the heavier type, they said this breed could do better scratching out a living on their rocky hillsides.

Guineas were great family "watch dogs" as they honked or squalled loud enough to wake the dead if anything strange dared come near. Their eggs were somewhat smaller than hen eggs, but they are no different in taste. They raised ducks and geese mainly for the feathers that made great warm "featherbeds" and pillows. The geese feathers were picked every month. Featherbeds in a cold house with no central heat were lightweight and exceptionally warm. They considered featherbeds necessary for every bed. A huge feather that hung on the wall by the fireplace swept the ashes off the hearth into the fire. Before pencils and "store-bought" pens, they filled feather quills with ink for writing.

The sisters petted and pampered their sheep. An interesting note is that none of the sheep would come near if someone were wearing pants-even if the sisters called the sheep. When the sheep came within view and saw someone wearing pants, they ran the other direction no matter how much the sisters tried to coax them to come near. Even putting down a trail of food would not persuade the sheep to come in.

When the Saturday Evening Post interview was underway, the photographer wanted a picture of the sheep. One of the girls called "sheepie, sheepie, sheepie," and one of the sheep came within sight. When it saw the photographer, it bolted and ran away. Consequently, no picture of sheep appeared in the article.

A farmer was considered privileged to own his own goats. They are not, however, the most amiable animals to have around. They can get into a lot of mischief including eating buttons off clothing, running inside the house, and standing on beds and furniture if given a chance. They climb atop practically anything. Farmers concluded that the by-product of the male mating goat is the most horrific odor on earth. This gave rise to the expression that something smelled like a Billy goat if it smelled really bad.

However, many considered goat milk a cure-all for digestive problems. Mountain people have believed for many years that goat milk is much better to drink than milk from cows. Some farmers owned a rare breed of fainting goats that fainted dead away for a few moments when they heard loud noises. We do not know which breed of goats the Walker Sisters owned.

The Walkers had at least one horse and as many as three mules at different times. They were seen leading a horse while in the fields looking for herbs ("yarbs.") Mules were preferred among mountain people as they were gentler, less spirited, easier to control, and perhaps cheaper. Horse thieves were a problem in the area. That one could hardly go more than three or four generations back without finding a horse thief sounds ludicrous today, but in those days without cars and telephones, a horse or mule was a necessity. In those days, stealing a horse or mule was a very serious crime. Without jail houses, a horse thief was punished by a brand of the letters "H T" on the cheek or hand.

Honeybees were a vital part of the Walkers' pioneer life. Bees not only pollinated the crops, but they also provided honey for food and medical uses. The Walkers sometimes traded their honey for molasses produced on other farms in the area. While we are unsure how the Walkers used their honey, some believed honey could remove cataracts and could kill bacteria such as typhoid, bronchi-pneumonia, abscesses, and dysentery. In fact, a doctor recently told me that physicians sometimes use honey to treat sores resulting from circulation problems. However, honey was dangerous for children younger one year old.

Robbing the bees was a somewhat dangerous job requiring much advance preparation to prevent bee stings. Mr. Walker robbed the bees for honey during his lifetime. Before special equipment became available, Mr. Walker would fill his mouth with water and honey, rear back, and spit it high into the air so that it fell on his head and shoulders. He did this to encourage the bees to gather the honey instead of stinging him.

Later, beekeepers used a smoker, which was about the size of a small coffee pot with a spout and a small opening at the top. When small rags were burned in the smoker, smoke enveloped the bees when the beekeeper pumped a moveable lever inside the smoker. The smoke subdued the bees and kept them from stinging the person robbing the hive.

When screen wire finally became available, beekeepers fastened it completely around a hat, making what they called a "bee face." The beekeeper could easily see through the bee face while subduing the greatly disturbed bees. I do not know which of the girls later undertook this job.

Wild animals included deer, black bear, bobcats, turkeys, wild boars and mountain lions. Bears were quite plentiful. My family told the story that my Uncle Levi Trentham, who owned a store at Elkmont, killed 69 bears in one year around 1890. He said the night before he went hunting he would dream where or how to find a bear. He said he followed the directions of those dreams.

In the later years, wild animals presented a real problem for the sisters. They had to guard against animals that would destroy sheep, goats, chickens and guineas, while watching out for rattlesnakes and copperheads. They fought off bears that ripped up their garden. They looked out for razorback hogs and chased foxes, hawks and weasels that killed their chickens. They had to put bells on their turkeys so hunters would not mistake them for wild turkeys.

Bears, panthers, wild boars, rattlesnakes and copperheads were the most dangerous animals they had to deal with. Groundhogs, opossums, skunks, muskrats, and weasels deserve honorable mention. Chiggers, wasps, hornets and yellow jackets caused a passel of trouble and aggravation.

Without news from the outside to discuss, old timers had more time to discuss nature and anything associated with their way of life. People often discussed wild animals and their encounters with them. Mountain people generally believed bears and panthers would not eat anything they did not kill. If a person lay down and pretended to be dead, the animal would not bother him.

My mother-in-law, Ida Jane Headrick Myers, who lived near the Walker Sisters' home, told a story about her encounter with a panther. When walking though the woods from the Little Cove School, where she taught as a very young woman, she realized a panther was stalking her. Knowing there was no way she could outrun the panther, she decided that lying on the ground was her only choice. The panther came up to her and covered her with leaves. She lived to tell this really wild tale.

People in the area also believed they could scare away bears if they made loud noises such as screaming. They sometimes carried a tin can partially filled with small rocks, which they shook vigorously if they encountered a bear. This sound usually caused the bear the run away. People said if the bear did not run, you were to run. If there were two of you, you only had to outrun the other person.

Mountain people believed that only men and wild boars did not have reflective eyes at night. With the reputation of wild boars, that was no compliment to man. The boars of the Smoky Mountains were so mean that neither man nor dog dared fight them. Unless a dog had on a special thick high collar, the boar could kill him with one swipe. Mountain folk believed the boar would hold a grudge against a man and would do as much damage as possible if mistreated. They believed wild boars intentionally tore down cooking pots outside. Boars could burrow, uproot and overturn like a bulldozer, outrun a deer, and climb like a goat. With commonly held beliefs of this type in the area, the Walker Sisters were particularly wary.

Farmers did not consider wolves to be a real problem. They commonly believed the noise of guns drove the wolves out of most of the Park environs. Only those who had a special rapport with wolves were in any way distressed by their absence. Many farmers were glad to see them go because they sometimes killed livestock.

Despite danger from wolves, however, some of the old timers were upset. Particularly those elders associated with tribal Indian culture believed that wolves were messengers of the spirit world. They were said to listen to the howls of wolves to gain insight and wisdom.

All family members had to deal with adversity. There were many ways to handle it. Mrs. Walker showed great ingenuity when dealing with a weasel. She heard one of her hens making an unusual noise. This hen was setting on eggs to hatch. When Mrs. Walker investigated, she found a weasel had attacked the hen. While attempting to remove the weasel, it latched onto her thumb. She simply walked to a nearby washtub, and thrust the weasel into the water. She knew that it would soon have to turn her loose or drown. Needless to say, the weasel drowned.

Little information exists about the snake den found under the back corners of the Walker Sisters' home after they became "famous." They told visitors never to go to that area because it was "snaky." Apparently, a space beneath the house made a good home for copperheads. One visitor I interviewed mentioned that the sisters talked about watching green snake venom coming out of a bite. They did not mention if the victim was a family member or an animal. At any rate, at least one time copperheads became such a problem that they asked the National Park Service to help them get rid of the snakes.

Wiley Oakley, a native of Gatlinburg, who was a well-known guide for tourists until his death in 1954 told about taking a group on a tour of the Smokies. This tour included a visit to the

Walkers' home. When they arrived, they found dead rattlesnakes in the front yard. Oakley asked Dan, one of the sons, if he had killed the snakes. Dan replied that he had, indeed, killed the snakes and that there were many others in the area.

In contrast, the black snakes, which stayed in the attic wrapped around the exposed rafters could be very frightening. One man, who spent many nights in the Walker home as a young boy, described his first experience seeing the black snakes looking down at him as he lay on the straw mattress. He instantly raced down the ladder attached to the wall and jumped in bed with his mother. He was very disappointed to be told that the snakes would not bother him. They were there to catch the mice. Afraid of being mistaken for a mouse, he said he did not sleep a wink all night. He said he saw the snakes every time his family visited. They did not attempt to bother him, but he was never able to sleep.

Dogs sometimes helped with the snake problem. However, they could receive bites as well. Fred Walker, 90-year-old nephew of the Sisters, said he had a dog named Old Ring. Old Ring spent as much as three hours holding a rattlesnake in place. Constantly barking, the dog chased round and round the snake, wearing out a ring or path. This would continue until Mr. Walker got his gun and shot the snake.

In later years, the Walker Sisters dramatically reduced the number of sheep and other farm animals because bears and other wild animals killed them. They obtained three dogs to help protect their animals. The dogs would have stayed outside sleeping in a dry place on the porch near the door. They proved to be absolutely unselfish friends for these isolated mountain women.

MEDICAL CARE

It is exceptional that all eleven of the Walker children reached maturity. The flu pandemic of 1918-1920 took the lives of 675,000 Americans. With childhood diseases of measles and mumps and epidemics of yellow fever and flu, infectious diseases were a constant threat. Mountain folk credited herbs and natural remedies with saving many lives.

John Walker boasted that throughout his entire life he had spent only fifty cents for the services of any medical doctor. He spent that money when his two sons developed measles while away at school. However, illness and accidents assuredly befell the family. Because of the absence of trained medical care, mountain families treated snakebites and other ills at home.

Those with a knowledge of mountain remedies administered herbs and potions with faith and ritual. Among the vegetables grown in the garden were the many medicinal herbs Mother Walker grew to keep the family healthy. These herbs included horseradish, catnip, boneset, Indian turnips, and peppermint. All of the sisters were also herb doctors.

While we are unsure of all the potions the Walker Sisters used, the following were common remedies in the area. The obnoxious weed, plantain, was considered a cure for mad dog and snakebite. After bruising or beating plantain leaves into a pulp, herbalists bound the leaves to the site of a bite. Tea made from peach leaves was and still is great for upset stomach and diarrhea. Reportedly, this tea contained the poison, cyanide, so they only took about 1/4 cup four times per day. Herbalists made a poultice of bruised peach leaves and applied it to stone bruises on the feet.

Placing a pan of cold water under a patient's bed was supposed to help cool the fever of typhoid. Ginseng was supposed to cure colic; boiled and sweetened sheep dung or "bullets" were supposed to "break-out" measles. Mountain folk used spider webs placed on raw wounds to stop bleeding. When someone's life was at stake, family members or friends repeated the Bible verse found in Ezekiel 16:6.

After removing the stinger of a bee, mountain herb doctors mixed salt with saliva in the palm of the hand and rubbed it vigorously on the sting. Beekeepers who still use this remedy claim it is better than any other remedy. Turpentine was used to treat a boil or carbuncle. Brown sugar or honey was supposed to stop cataracts. For constipation or "locked bowels," May-apple root was boiled down, mixed with flour, and eaten with sugar.

Many mountain people drank Sassafras tea to thin the blood. Sassafras roots also made a wonderful drink. In the spring, parents lined up all members of the family and administered a spoonful of sulphur mixed with molasses as a tonic. After applying camphorated oil to prevent burning the skin, mountain doctors recommended dabbing lamp oil (kerosene) on a wool cloth and placing it on the chest for pneumonia. Boneset and catnip tea were alternative remedies. While convalescing after a bout with pneumonia, one of the sisters added, "I nearly took a back set when I got to knocking about." Translation: She nearly had a setback when she became active again.

Old-timers said ginseng, a very popular locally grown herb, was "good for everything that ails you." These ailments included asthma, coughs, boils, internal diseases, palsy, nervousness, and memory problems. Some also considered ginseng to act as an aphrodisiac. Called in the mountain vernacular "sang," it appeared to be a cure-all. The older roots, if shaped like a human body, were very highly treasured. Ginseng brought 42 cents per pound in 1881.

The chief healing potion for the girls was their Uncle Charley Walker's secret liniment that used Indian turnips and May-apple root. It was rubbed on the temple for fainting or headaches, on the chest for coughing, and on the muscles for stiffness. In fact, devotees used it for almost everything external. Some who used it described it as being as "hot as hell's hinges" and mighty powerful.

Before the days of tetanus shots, a woman came to our home in the mountains with blood poisoning in her badly swollen arm. My father mixed equal parts of sulfur, gunpowder, and alum. She took orally what would lie on a dime. Then he applied a poultice combining the mixture with vinegar. Much improved, she went home within three days.

Some people credit brown sugar with curing cataracts. A hospital administrator told me about a woman sent home to wait for cataract surgery. When she returned, the cataracts were missing. At first, the woman refused to tell what she had done.

After much urging, she confessed that an old mountain woman told her to put brown sugar in her eyes. The hospital administrator added that the drops given after cataract surgery contain brown sugar in solution.

Mrs. Walker's mother was a midwife who taught Margaret Jane while introducing her to mountain remedies. We have no evidence that the sisters carried on the midwife tradition. Midwives used a birthing stool in those days. The method of "sniffing" assisted in the delivery or birthing a new baby. When it was determined that the baby was ready to be born, someone put snuff on a plate and would blow it into the expectant mother's face. This was supposed to put her mind on something else to relieve her during the most painful part of the birthing process.

Midwives were very important to mountain families. They received little formal training, but they provided a great service. My mother was a midwife for many years. She participated in a training course of about two weeks and helped to deliver 195 babies without the death of a baby or a mother. She sometimes stayed with a family for two to three days. For her services, she was paid five dollars. Often when she saw poor conditions in the home, she returned home to gather items to take back to the family.

When I was about two years old, I raised such a fuss when she was leaving to help with a delivery that the father of the baby had to bring me with them to his house. Until his death, he reminded me that he had to carry me on his hip around the mountain so my mother could deliver his child. My older sisters always dreaded hearing the knock at the door in the middle of the night asking for my mother. They knew they would have to get up early to do the cooking for our family.

A common treatment for rattlesnake bites was to bath the site with a mixture of lamp oil, turpentine and Roger's liniment, which locals purchased from "drummers" or traveling salesmen. This mixture was then placed in a very small-mouth bottle and held against the skin at the site of the bite. This treatment helped to draw out the venom. Those who saw the treatment said they could nearly see the poison coming out of the skin.

When dogs were victims of snakebites, farmers might also apply a strong brew of cocklebur leaves to the site. When a dog in a coma received this treatment, it is said he would be up within an hour seeming no worse for the experience. Dock leaves were still another remedy used for snakebites and boils.

Maybe we mountain folk were right when we believed a snake did not die until sundown. Jim Shelton, married to Caroline Walker Shelton, told of cutting a rattlesnake's head off. Later his hand was close to the headless neck and it struck him on the wrist. Toxicologists report that 15% of rattlesnake bites they treat come from snakes that have been dead at least several minutes. Really dead: shot, bludgeoned, and even decapitated. It seems that biting is a reflex action that takes a while to shut down.

Few considered cancer a major disease in the early years, possibly because people did not live as long as they do today. Some old time cancer cures included drinking a tea of red clover blooms three times a day for stomach cancer and inhaling apple brandy for lung cancer. Pokeroot mixed with zinc chloricum was supposed to remove skin cancer. Eating at least three almonds per day was said to prevent cancer.

Even today in Tennessee, a controversy continues over the use of another natural remedy, flax oil, as a cure for cancer. A man given six months to live with prostate cancer, began using freshly processed flax seed oil and was still alive ten years later. Doctors and family members expected a woman cancer victim, who weighed only sixty pounds, to die. She credited tea made from the wood pulp of the dogwood tree with curing her. Others claim these remedies will not work.

Dentists were very rare, and most people never visited one. Dentists introduced the idea of preventative dental care long after the Walker Sisters died. Mountain folk cleaned their teeth with a brush made of a birch twig. After peeling back about ½ inch of the bark, they rubbed the stem around in the mouth to soften the bristles. They used a mixture of baking soda with a small amount of salt as a dentifrice.

Families solved dental problems at home. They considered dental caries inevitable. Toothache was generally treated with oil of cloves. Cavities in teeth remained until a toothache became too painful to ignore. Once the pain was too great, they removed the tooth. Families kept tooth-pullers, made somewhat like pliers, for that purpose.

Many families did not have traditional tooth-pullers, so they used a procedure called "tooth-jumping." They used tooth-jumping to remove children's baby teeth or abscessed adult teeth. The person experienced in the art of tooth-jumping placed a chisel just under the gum of the offending tooth. He would then flick the wrist, hitting the chisel with a hammer. The tooth would jump out. Sometimes the patient claimed they never felt any pain with this method.

The Walker Sisters used many mountain remedies. We cannot know all of them. However, we know they remained healthy and active throughout their lives.

CHURCH AND SCHOOL

Schooling for the Walker children was consistent with the education offered to all mountain children. Teachers and fellow classmates considered the Walker children above average students. The girls went through the sixth grade at the Little Greenbriar School. William Wylie and John Henry went to Wearwood School in Wears Valley and then attended Murphy College in Sevierville. I believe Murphy College was located where the Church of God children's home is now located. Both brothers later taught at Little Greenbriar School.

Until the Little Greenbriar school was built, parents who could raise 10 or 15 dollars cooperated to hire someone who had legible handwriting, a blue-black speller, and knew 'rithmic' to teach their children. With approximately sixty families living in and around the Metcalf Bottoms and Little Greenbriar communities, the families recognized a real need for a permanent school building and teacher. In 1880, they petitioned Sevier County to establish a school in their community. The county agreed to provide a teacher if the residents provided a school building.

My great uncle, William Gilbert "Gib" Abbott donated the land for a school building, and my maternal grandfather Ephraim Ogle donated the huge poplar logs to build the walls. My grandfather also furnished the poplar slabs, which they split to build the puncheon floor.

William Walker agreed to hire out his oxen to haul the logs to the building site. Because Mr. Walker did the hauling, some of the men performed work for him to pay for the service. A team of two oxen could pull only one log at a time. Workers placed one end of a log on the rear of a strong wagon. The other end dragged the ground.

My grandfather, along with uncle Gib Abbott, John Walker and Henry Clabough were selected as "corner men" responsible for notching and fitting the logs at each corner. They called these corners "dove-tail" joints. These corner men had helpers. John Walker's seventeen-year-old son, Thomas Walker, helped his father. Bill Stinnett, son of Ben and Millie Stinnett, helped my grandfather. Bill Watson helped Henry Clabough. I do not know the name of Abbott's helper. A worker considered it a mark of distinction to be selected as a corner man because it required great skill to fit those corners so that water would not seep in and destroy the building.

My great-grandfather, Billie Ogle, father of Ephraim, was a very old man at this time. However, he wanted to help. So, he split the shingle laths from the straight grain oak and bolted the boards to cover the roof. Billie Abbott helped to rivet the bolts. The walls were built five logs high with straight poles cut for the rafters. The first benches were made of poplar slabs with four legs and no backs. In later years, a second set of benches with backs was made of dressed lumber. Students still had no desks. The third set of benches with both backs and desks are in the school building today.

The children, who were eager for a school building, helped with construction. The girls carried boards for the roof to the ladder. The boys carried them up the ladder to the men who were putting the roof on the building. The women of the community prepared lunch for the "workin'." To celebrate completion of the building, preacher John Abbott stood on his head.

On New Years day, 1882 teacher and students met for the first class. Some of the children walked as far as nine miles to attend school. Richard Walker, son of James Thomas and Ida Stinnett Walker, walked each morning from his home on Indian Camp

Little Greenbriar School as seen today. Courtesy of Southland Books.

Branch to build a fire at the school. He received five cents for his service. Wood was stacked on each side of the front door of the school. A water bucket and dipper supplied drinking water for the children. Each child drank from the same dipper.

As agreed, Sevier County supplied the teacher, Richard Perryman. He received a $1.25 fee for each pupil who attended the school. The total amount of fees received determined the length of the school term. In the beginning, each term was seldom longer than two months. The school term gradually lengthened to nine months.

The cold winter months of December, January and February were best suited for school because parents did not need their children to work the crops. The teacher taught six subjects: reading, arithmetic, Tennessee History, U.S. History, spelling and writing. Students competed in spelling bees on Fridays afternoons. The last student left standing who correctly spelled all the words was the winner.

My mother, born in 1886, was eligible to attend this school in 1892. She stated that she had only a slate on which to write her lessons. A cook stove heated the building. My mother had to sit so far from the heat that her heels became frostbitten. She said the treatment for her feet was the acid extracted after boiling a hornet's nest. George Melton, who was born and reared near the school, told how he and others went to school barefooted when frost was on the ground. He said their toes "were as red as turkey snouts when they arrived." In 1907, Jim Shelton made a picture at the school in which all nine children on the front row were barefooted.

When nurses and doctors started coming to local schools, giving shots for typhoid, diphtheria, etc, many of the students refused to take the shots. When they saw that the students were still alive the next day, they agree to take them.

Schoolchildren sometimes had head lice and a condition called "itch." Both conditions were very contagious. To treat head lice, parents doused the child's head with kerosene. If someone merely touched a book that someone with itch owned, he could expect to get it. To cure the "itch," mothers mixed sulphur with hog's lard and smeared it over the entire body. The child then stood naked before a hot fire to bake the sulphur into the body. Because the sulphur odor was so strong, all clothing and bedding had to be burned if the sulphur touched it. Nothing would remove the odor.

My own family had to deal with these issues as well. My Mother and one of my sisters once contracted the itch. For treatment, we locked them in our smoke house and forgot them. The wood button latch was on the outside of the building. To avoid suffocating, they had to lift the trap door into the dugout area under the smokehouse to let in some fresh air.

Even though children were eager to have a school, some students misbehaved. If a child feigned illness to keep from going to school, he was given a dose of castor oil. Parents said if the child were not really sick, he would be. Students made pop guns to shoot paper wads from elder bushes. The elder bushes had a large inside core. Punishment meted out for misbehavior was very different to today's practice. Punishment consisted of requiring a student to stand on one foot, place his or her nose in a circle drawn on the blackboard, or sit on a stool in the front corner of the room wearing a dunce cap.

One of the students wrote the following sentiments regarding one of the teachers: "Lord of love, Look down from above and pity us poor scholars. They found a fool to teach our school and paid him fifty dollars!"

Herman Matthews, the last teacher of this school in 1935-36, recalled how it began to snow one day. By 2:00 p.m., he decided it was best to send the children home while they could still make it. He then walked to Wears Valley, a distance of five or more miles, where he was boarding at the time. His rubber boots reached halfway to his knees. The snow came over the tops at times. The snow continued all night, reaching 24 to 30 inches. He remained out of school at least four weeks because the snow stayed on the ground so long.

The school building was also used for church worship services. At the first service all the four preachers present had an opportunity to speak. Because he was the oldest and he helped to build the school building, John Stinnett spoke first. The fact that he stood on his head when it was finished showed the joy he experienced to have the building completed.

By 1924, church attendance was too great for the size of the school building. Tine Metcalf (when I was growing up everyone pronounced it Madcap) donated the land adjoining the school property to build a church. I have found no information about the actual construction of this building.

Mrs. Walker, their mother, was originally a Methodist. When she converted to the same church as her husband, all the Walker family attended the Primitive Baptist church where they attended nearly every service. People often called these churches Hardshell Baptist churches. Primitive Baptists believed in foot-washing and total immersion for baptism. Communion consisted of grape juice instead of wine. Some Primitive churches also practiced snake handling, but I do not remember hearing about it in our immediate area.

I never attended a "foot-washing" so I cannot describe what occurs. However, before I was born, a particular man spent many nights at our house en route to his church foot-washing ceremonies. No one ever charged for overnight stays, which included evening and morning meals. Eventually, my father grew tired of his repeated visits. As was the custom, this visitor left his shoes by the fireside to keep them warm for the next morning. After he went to bed, my father put soot from the chimney into his shoes. No doubt, by the time he walked to church the next day the soot had ground onto his feet, which must have looked as if he had not bathed for weeks. This visitor never returned for free overnight lodging.

Foot-washings and baptisms were sometimes all-day affairs. Baptismal services took place in the river, where the water was "deep enough to completely immerse the candidate yet not deep enough to drown the minister." Baptisms often took place when the temperature was almost zero. However, we never heard that anyone died from such exposure. If the weather was good after these ceremonies or during hymn-singings, families enjoyed "dinner on the ground" in which everyone brought dishes of food to share.

The Walker family played an important role in the Little Greenbriar Church. Two of the Walker brothers, John and Wylie, served as Superintendents of the Sunday School. Jim Shelton, Caroline's husband, also served in that position.

The preacher came from Forks of the River (where we lived.) When he arrived at the Greenbriar Church, he rang the church bell to let his congregation know to come to the church for services. The bell lost its tongue (clapper), I understand.

Church members had little money for materials or repairs. Many churches had services only during the day because they could not afford to buy coal oil for lamps. Ministers sometime quoted the Bible verses indicating that it was easier for a camel to go through the eye of a needle than for a rich man to enter the kingdom of heaven. People interpreted this to mean that people should stay poor or that poverty and grace went hand in hand. Perhaps ministers did this to make churchgoers feel better about their plight.

It is interesting to know the atmosphere of the mountain churches. The church at Little Greenbriar would hardly have been different. Few ministers attended seminary. They relied on topics they considered relevant to daily life. They condemned moving picture shows, card playing, mixed public bathing, and social riding in autos. Dancing, use of profanity, idle words, breaking the Sabbath, use of cosmetics, smoking, and cooking on Sunday pretty much covered the ministers' messages.

Ministers often preached on the subject of clothing they considered too revealing. One church erected a curtain around the choir section so the ankles of female choir members were not exposed. Proper women did not cross their legs in public; they could cross their ankles, however. Women were careful not to cook, plant flowers, or sew on Sunday. Sunday was the day to visit the neighbor, rest, or catch up on the news and gossip. In fact, there was a saying that what you sew on Sunday, you pick out with your nose on Monday. Men discussed whether it was sinful to help a farm animal that had fallen into a hole on Sunday.

Churches usually had an "amen corner." During the service, people who agreed with the minister's comments would loudly say "amen." Members of the congregation most likely to agree sat in an area together. When ministers talked about revealing clothing, older women sat in the "amen corner" while nursing their babies in church and cast disapproving glances at the low necklines of offenders wearing "modern dress."

With few exceptions, the people were deeply religious. Many arose in the early morning saying: "I will lift up mine eyes unto the hills from whence cometh my help, my help cometh from the Lord." Honesty was very important to most mountain residents.

A very common statement in many books was "Steal not this book, for fear of shame, for in this book is the owners name, for when you die the Lord will say, where is that book you took away?"

The Walker Sisters took all of this very seriously. They always sat together in the "amen corner" at church. They lived their lives in a way they believed would bring them no criticism. Someone once asked the girls if they thought Heaven would condone dancing. One of them replied, "You can risk it if you like, but don't do it here."

Of all the comments about the Walker Sisters, I heard only one that I would consider negative. It involved their views of right and wrong. It seems that a young man they had known during their youth had spent some time "sowing his wild oats." They were aware of some of these incidents, and they strongly disapproved. He changed his life style, became a Christian, and felt that he should become a minister. When the congregation voted to license or ordain him as a minister, the sisters voted against him. The church body, accepting his change of life style, voted and ordained him anyway. When he was preaching at services they attended, they would loudly pat their feet or sometimes get up and leave the church. Right or wrong, they apparently never forgave his past indiscretions.

Until the late 1930's it was not unusual for someone to shout during church services. A church member shouted when he or she became overwhelmed with what the minister said or was overcome with the "Power of the Spirit." During one of the services in a nearby church, a woman was "shouting" when the elastic holding her panties broke. She promptly stepped out of them and tucked them aside as if nothing had happened. She shouted just as loudly: "Praise the Lord, it don't matter no how!"

Young people used that quote as a great "by-word" for months afterward when some questionable or unusual situation arose.

My mother told us when she was a young girl she mocked a woman who shouted in church. After quite a display my mother was struck to the ground and was paralyzed for some time before she recovered her ability to move. She assumed this was a warning that she was making sport of something that was genuinely spiritual.

At the end of services at the Little Greenbriar church, everyone sang: "God be with you 'til we meet again." Everyone went down to the altar and shook hands with everyone else. Maybe because life was so uncertain there was hardly a dry eye in the church.

Hymn singing and Old Harp singing were very important to local residents, including the Walker Sisters. Each of the sisters sang soprano and were said to have very good voices. In Old Harp singing, singers sat in four groups facing the center of the room. Each person took turns leading the singing. The congregation first sang the shaped notes of the song (fa, sol, la, mi). Then they sang all the words. Different voices repeated or delayed singing different phrases.

Very few churches could afford the expense of pianos and organs. Song leaders used tuning forks, tuning pipes or guitars to get the correct pitch for the songs. Some of the favorite songs in those days were "The Old Account Was Settled Long Ago," "We'll Work 'Til Jesus Comes," "Sweet By and By," and "I'm Pressing On the Upward Way."

Words for a favorite song are written below:

> Brethren, we have met to worship
> And adore the Lord our God;
> Will you pray with all your power?
> While we try to preach the word?
> All is vain unless the spirit
> Of the holy one comes down;
> Brethren pray and holy manna
> Will be showered all around.

After the church at Little Greenbriar was abandoned and the building destroyed, the Walker Sisters attended Headrick's Chapel in Wears Valley. Jim Shelton, sister Caroline's husband, was very good to drive them anywhere they wanted to go.

I received conflicting reports about what happened to the church building located close to the Little Greenbriar School. Therefore, I cannot say with any certainly what happened to it. One report was that the Park Service demolished it. Some think it went to the Valley View Church in Wears Valley. While some of the people who lived at Elkmont say their church was moved to the Happy Hollow, piece by piece; others say it was the Elkmont School that went to Happy Hollow. The most credible report I found leads me to believe it was moved to Happy Hollow.

No matter what happened to the church at Little Greenbriar, it was a meaningful part of the lives of those who attended services there.

SOCIAL AND CIVIC ACTIVITIES

The chief social activities for the Walker family were church-related. Those who knew them said the Sisters never missed a church service. Families focused on outside activities only after gathering and storing all the crops and cutting and stacking all the firewood for winter. Everyone worked hard but had time to play, sing, read the Bible or take part in family picnics.

Mr. Walker was very strict regarding social events in the community. When invited to parties, the sisters said they had "not much mind to such follies." However, they attended some social events. These events may have included making popcorn and pulling candy. Work parties such as apple peeling, corn-shuckings, bean-breakings, and pea-shellings were also popular. When they were older, friends brought ice cream equipment with dry ice to make ice cream.

Story telling was an important part of family life. Families sat around the fire at night and listened as family members or guests told about personal events, tall tales, or "haint" (haunt) tales. Parents often passed on stories about values and religion. The chief games played in the home were checkers and fox and geese. In fox and geese, buttons designated the foxes while grains of corn represented geese. Fox and geese was played on a checkerboard. The rules were similar to the rules for checkers. Players removed any "jumped" piece from the board. When either player lost all his pieces, he lost the game.

Music was also a part of life for the Walker Sisters. As mentioned previously, they enjoyed attending hymn singings and Old Harp singings at their church. Jim Shelton, Caroline's husband, was a self-taught banjo and guitar "picker." He tutored Dan Walker, their nephew, to become one also.

The Walker Sisters greeted old friends who visited them with a curtsy. If guests arrived during hot weather, they offered them a drink of water from their wooden water bucket along with a gourd dipper with which to drink it.

The Walker Sisters were gracious hosts. However, they were assertive when it came to their own needs. A visitor once asked the sisters if they would mind if he smoked. Margaret replied, "It'll only make two people sick, you and me."

Of the eleven Walker children, four or five married and two of the five sisters who stayed at home were engaged to marry. "Courting" became a part of the Walker family life, but it could be difficult in that setting. In those days if a young man owned a lantern, a gun, a dog, salt, a frying pan and some sour dough starter he was considered ready to look for a wife.

When boys went courting, they sometimes slicked their hair down with hog's lard. A young man came to a girl's home after he finished all his work. In many homes parents supplied a "timer" to tell a young man when to leave. Parents lit a candle. When it burned down, it was time for the young man to go. I wondered how many blew out the candle and re-lit it to gain more time.

Few opportunities were available for courting when the Walker Sisters were young. There were no movies or cars for dating. Young people attended candy-pulling and corn-shucking parties. If a boy found a red ear of corn at a corn-shucking, he could kiss one of the girls. However, Mr. Walker did not allow his daughters to attend those parties. They also would not have attended the parties in which musicians played music while young and old danced all night.

Young men complained their only opportunity to talk to girls was to wait outside the church to request the opportunity to walk a girl home. If a boy asked a girl out and she gave him a sour look, she did not have to say anything. If she kicked him in the shins, that too told him "no." It was called "breaking your leg" among the boys.

It was also difficult for young men to travel to distant communities where they would find non-relatives to meet and marry. Poor roads and the lack of transportation were great hindrances. Young men also found that their counterparts in other communities discouraged their visits. Sometimes they threw rocks at visiting bachelors to force them to leave their young women alone.

Some families held open houses for eligible young men to meet their female offspring. People in the community considered the girl who attracted the greatest number of young men the most popular-- even if she did not find a husband among them. It seems unlikely that the Walker family held such open houses for their daughters.

Older people cautioned young people about marrying a first cousin. They said if a genetic disorder existed in the family, it could be multiplied if they had children. However, with so few families in the area, it was hard to find someone who was not at least distantly related.

Before his death, Mr. Walker had a very predictable and satisfying social outlet. His social life revolved around joining the local men on Saturday down at the country store for fun and jokes. The store was located at the Metcalf Bottoms, slightly more than a mile from the Walker home.

Peddlers or drummers brought news and stories to the area. Mr. Walker gathered news of the outside world as he sat and chatted about world and local affairs with local men. Pity the passing of the general store of those days where the men gathered around the old pot-bellied stove to whittle, and 'chaw and jaw.' Story telling and stretching the truth was at its best. Some men were said to be such liars that they had to get someone to call their hogs to eat. For some it was a refuge for men who had been shooed out of the house so the womenfolk could get the work done. The men were constantly setting up one another for jokes.

And, they told jokes to one another. The type of jokes they told may be represented by one I remember from high school, which involved girls swimming in the nude. Some local boys came along and sat on the riverbank until the girls got disgusted with having to stay underwater for so long. One girl found a dishpan in the river, held it up in front of her torso and started telling the boys what she thought. One boy listened for a moment and said, "Yes, we know what you think. You think that dishpan has a bottom in it."

The men surely discussed the occasional train wrecks of the Little River Lumber Company, weather, farming, politics of the day, and the reign of terror of the White Caps in Sevier County.

The White Caps were an organized group of criminals who terrorized the citizens around Sevierville during a four-year period in the late 1890's. Residents called them White Caps because their head coverings were similar to caps worn by members of the Ku Klux Klan. During that time thirty or more people were killed because of grudges or just general cruelty. The rein of terror ended with the hanging of two White Cap members, Pleas Wynn and Catlett Tipton. My father attended the hanging of Wynn and Tipton in Sevierville. He said the crowd was so great that he had to climb a tree to watch. He said, however, he would never willingly witness something like that again.

Beginning in 1886 and continuing for several years, the races between brothers Alf and Bob Taylor, who competed against each other for governor of Tennessee, were very entertaining. One brother was a Democrat and the other a Republican. They traveled together and debated one another. Their mother had them sign a pledge stating that if either became angry he would drop out of the race.

Both the brothers were entertaining speakers. One of their often-repeated stories told of their being at a dance, celebrating Robert E. Lee's birthday. They said, "The fiddles were playing and everyone was swinging their corners (dancing.) The boys started slapping each other on the back as they swung. One boy was knocked down when slapped too hard. His brother shot that feller. That feller's brother cut the other feller's throat. That feller that was knocked down took his knife and cut that feller's liver out. The old man of the house, got mad, ran upstairs, got his shotgun and turned both barrels loose on that crowd. I saw there was going to be trouble, so I left."

Men also discussed local events. No doubt, local crimes and resulting punishments were common topics. Until the 1890's Sevierville had a public whipping post at which one man received 39 lashes for stealing a handkerchief. A woman received nine lashes for stealing three ounces of sewing thread. One woman's crime of stealing cloth from a loom was uncovered at a church meeting. When she moved, her skirt rose high enough to show her petticoat. Every weaver knew her own woven material. The weaver sitting next to her recognized her own cloth. The female thief became an outcast and her husband was known thereafter as "Pitticoat Jim."

During those days Justices of the Peace, better known as JP's, held court one Saturday of each month. If two people had a dispute, they came to the JP's home or to a school building where the JP decided the issue if possible. If the JP failed to settle the differences, the two people had a fistfight. The one who lost the fight lost the case.

In addition to voting and building schools and churches, men of the day had other civic responsibilities. Every able-bodied man between the ages of 21 and 45 was required to work five to eight days per year on the roads or pay up to $6 for extra days. No doubt, the men at the store planned and discussed these workdays.

Holidays allowed family members to enjoy each other's company and escape from the constant farm work. There were always special meals at Christmas and Easter, but most women prepared a special meal every Sunday. (You never knew when the preacher was coming home with you for Sunday dinner.)

All families of that area celebrated Christmas with what means was available. They usually selected a tall white pine, cedar or hemlock tree to decorate. Colored paper cutouts, popcorn on strings, and sweet gum balls dipped in soapsuds trimmed the trees. There was an abundance of mistletoe and holly with beautiful red berries for decorations.

The Yule Log or huge back-stick in the fireplace played a major role during the Christmas season. The log was soaked in the river or creek for a few days before Christmas. As long as it burned in the fireplace, menfolk of the family had to do no farm work. I presume the women had to feed the animals, milk the cows, and perform the other chores all this time.

In the very early days, families with Indian ancestry would put out the fire, clean the fireplace, and go to a community center at the beginning of a new year. Here the chief or priest started a new fire with a piece of the old Yule log. Each family took fire-coals with which to start a new fire in their hearth for the New Year. This had a beautiful symbolism because with this act everyone was to forgive grudges and old hurts and never mention them again.

In my family and many mountain households, parents told children that the cows knelt at midnight on Christmas Eve and that they sometimes spoke or communicated through a type of cow-to-child telepathy. I never went to the barn to see for myself. In addition, they believed that water sometimes turned to wine at midnight. Another midnight Christmas tradition involved burning a piece of cedar at midnight, a sort of incense.

The mistletoe tradition was as common to early mountain families as it is today. At that time, a young man picked a berry from the mistletoe for each kiss. When he had removed each berry, no more kisses were allowed. Gradually the berries remained with the mistletoe. As long as the girl stood under the mistletoe, she was fair game. Traditionally, mistletoe was credited with mysterious powers. It was said to be sacred, to assure fertility, and offered protection from evil.

Any young girl not kissed under the mistletoe would not get married the following year. Being considered an "Old-Maid" was disgraceful. Because they did not go to parties as young women, the Walker Sisters probably did not participate in many of the Christmas traditions associated with mistletoe. Many others in the mountains took full advantage.

Apples, oranges, nuts and candies were always part of Christmas gift giving. Parents usually gave a hand-made toy to each child. Children always hung up stockings (usually a sock the child actually wore) for Santa. If the child had been particularly bad, a knot was tied in his stocking and he got nothing. I heard of only one child of our area who found a knot tied in his sock. He cried so loudly and long that the parents had to give in and give him a gift to stop the crying.

One of the favorite Christmas stories came with the early settlers. In a faraway land, people believed that if someone made a truly sacrificial offering at the church, the angels rang some beautiful-sounding bells. However, an entire generation had come and gone and the bells had not rung. So the King of this distant land declared for the upcoming Christmas that everyone should bring the most generous gift possible to the church. The king said he would also bring his gift.

Two young brothers lived a great distance from the church. Their family was very poor. Each boy managed to save a small silver coin for an offering. Early on Christmas Eve, holding their coins tightly, they started the long walk to the city. It was bitterly cold and they had gone a short distance when it began to snow very hard. Hand in hand, with their shabby clothes wrapped tightly around them, they trudged on. The sun had set, and the snow was getting very deep.

Suddenly the older boy stumbled on something huddled in the snow. Kneeling, he found an old woman, nearly frozen, but still alive. He began to rub her hands and face. He wrapped his coat around her until her breathing became more regular. In the distance, huge crowds moved toward the church. The older boy, still working with the old woman, told his brother to go alone to the church. He handed him his coin saying, "Here is my offering. But I must stay here until some of the people leaving the church can help."

By the time the little boy arrived at the church the entire crowd was leaving. Everyone brought a gift. The King himself had taken the magnificent crown off his head and placed it on the altar. Still the bells had not rung. Shyly making his way through the departing crowd, the little boy placed both coins on the altar. Suddenly the most beautiful bells rang out with tones never heard before. Looking back toward the church the king was able to see a small shabbily dressed child leaving the altar. Elders told stories of this type as reminders of how everyone was expected to act.

Church members might enact a special church program at Easter. Parents always tried to have a new article of clothing for the children. There were always Easter egg hunts. In my own family, Mary Ann Reagan Ogle, my grandmother, hid the eggs for us to hunt. This was one of my favorite memories of her.

Mountain families also enjoyed celebrating Halloween. Door-to-door trick-or-treating did not start where we lived until the early 1950's. Young people sometimes wore costumes to Halloween parties, but the Walker Sisters probably would not have attended. I remember one Halloween party at the Pi Beta Phi School in Gatlinburg when I was in 6th or 7th grade. This would have been around 1930 before we moved from the Park. We "bobbed" for apples in a tub of water. I remember winning first prize for my costume. My sister cut out eyes, nose, and a mouth in a pillowcase and outlined these in black. She stuffed the corners of the pillowcase for ears and wrapped a sheet around me. When I won, I did not want to admit who I was because I had told my teacher, Stella Huff, I could not attend.

Halloween pranksters presented a challenge to the older folks. They often enjoyed turning over outhouses. Another prank they enjoyed was to disassemble a farm wagon and reassemble it across the roof of a public building. This happened to my father's wagon when my youngest brother was supposed to go by wagon to Walden's Creek the following day to get a load of wood.

Primarily, however, young celebrants overturned outhouses. One man grew tired of such shenanigans. He moved his outhouse structure just behind the actual pit. He created a temporary cover over the pit. When the pranksters came to overturn the building, they found themselves hip deep in the existing pit. That was the end of pranks at that location.

The Walker Sisters were somewhat superstitious. If you entered their house by one door, they made sure you exited by that same door. They believed it was unlucky not to do so. They did not allow anyone to open an umbrella inside the house. We are unsure what other superstitions they may have believed or followed. However, some of the more common superstitions of their time are listed below:

- Seeing a bird in the house portends the impending death of a family member.
- Singing at the dinner table was bad luck.
- Carrying a buckeye in your pocket brings good luck and prevents arthritis.
- August 27 was the most "poisonest" day of the year. (I am unsure what that was all about. It may have had something to do with dog days when many believed wounds would not heal if they were exposed to dew on the ground.)
- The number of stars seen in a ring around the moon tells how many days until rain.
- If rain falls while the sun is shining, it will rain at that time tomorrow.
- When killing a snake hang him belly side up to make it rain.
- If the wind shows the underside of leaves, rain will fall soon.
- Cricket chirps can tell the temperature: (Count the number of chips in 14 seconds and add 40 to give you degrees in Fahrenheit.)
- Bees come home and fish surface before a storm.

- If you catch cistern water during any month that has an "R" in it, especially the first four months of year "wiggle tails" will grow in it. (That was when mosquitoes were hatching. We put kerosene on top of the water to kill them and caught water in the water tank or cistern the year round.)
- Some old timers believed if they heard thunder in January there would be frost in May.
- If the new moon will hold water (tipped like a bowl), the next two weeks will be wet. If the new moon tilts so that it will not hold water, the next two weeks will be dry.

A death in the family provided a very different experience for any mountain family. Someone tolled the church bell once for each year of life of the deceased. Everyone in the community stopped what they were doing to count this number to determine rather accurately who had just passed. Neighbors could judge more easily if they knew someone that age was seriously ill. After the bells tolled, someone from each family often went to the cemetery to confirm who had died and helped to dig the grave. Other neighbors constructed the coffin. Women in the community began preparing food to take to the bereaved family.

When someone died, relatives immediately split open the feather pillow of the deceased searching for a "crown." This was a woven mass of feathers resembling a bun, soft to the touch but quite heavy. If the feathers were woven into a complete circle, it was proof that the deceased was going to an eternal reward in heaven. If they found a crown, everyone rejoiced.

My theory is that a circle of this type had nothing to do with an eternal resting place. I believe that with many months of use feathers naturally matted, forming this type of circle. One old-timer best explained the scarcity of these "crowns" in later days when he said, "There jus 'ain't as many people that's deservin' 'em these days."

Until funeral homes and morticians became common in the 1920's and 1930's, family and neighbors assumed responsibility for preparation of the body and burial. If the deceased was male, the men laid him out on a cooling board. If female, the women performed that task. They placed a cloth saturated with camphor on the face to prevent darkening. Nickels were place over the eyes to keep them closed. They placed a strap around the head to hold the chin in place. All of this was done at no cost to the family.

It was the tradition for someone to "sit up" with the dead. Family members took turns remaining awake and in the same room with the body during the night. The burial usually took place within twenty-four hours, especially in warm weather. A funeral service usually took place in the home. Unless a minister was close, a member of the family said a few words about the life of the deceased, read some scripture from the Bible, and said a prayer. After the service, the pallbearers carried the casket to the family cemetery plot, usually very close to the home. For longer journeys, they used a wagon. After a graveside service, everyone returned to the home to eat the abundant food, begin the mourning, and catch up with neighbors and relatives.

With poor communication, distant family members or friends would not learn of a death until after the funeral occurred. A letter edged in black notified them. At that time, if you received a letter edged in black, you knew before opening it that someone had died.

TRAVEL AND COMMUNICATIONS

Between 1900 and 1930 the process of modernization began in earnest with road building, telephones, and electricity eventually supplied by the Tennessee Valley Authority. Before that time, travel and communication were very difficult in East Tennessee. Most travel consisted of walking or riding a horse or mule.

Taking products to market presented a challenge for farmers who had surplus crops or livestock. Before automobiles, there were annual animal drives from this area to other states. The Walker Sisters never went the entire route but helped to get the participants on their way. Before the coming of the Park, cattle, ducks, turkeys, and hogs were driven to North Carolina, South Carolina, and Georgia.

The drivers or herders could go only about eight miles per day. Then they often had trouble finding a spot to camp where the animals could receive food and water and a place to rest or roost. Much of the animal food had to be carried with them. After selling the animals, the crew would stop on the way back and pay the board or lodging bill at places they stayed on the way to market.

For some reason, herders placed cows first in line in the drive. Perhaps it was because they were more controllable. Those who drove the herds refused to feed cattle green grass for a few days prior to the drive to avoid the "mess" in the trails. The cattle had brands, cuts, or splits in their ears to identify the owners.

Thousands of wild turkeys roamed the woods. They were herded to market in groups of 500 to 600. A master gobbler gobbled and strutted his stuff on the trail. Horsemen kept the flock in line with long whips with red flannel rags on the end.

Domestic hogs and wild boars, however, proved to be the greatest problems in these massive drives. Taking part in the drives was new to them, of course. Squealing animals went in every direction when the drivers said "Suey!" Drivers used prods to direct them where to go. One today can hardly believe that between 150,000 and 175,000 hogs were driven up the French Broad River every year between 1830 and 1840. By the time the Walker Sisters were children these numbers had declined. In fact, because Tennessee was the greatest corn-producing state and because farmers raised so many hogs, it became known as the "Hog and Hominy" state. It held that nickname until after the War of 1812, when it became the Volunteer State.

Women did not ride astraddle their mules. They wore so many petticoats it was not possible to straddle the animal. The practice was also considered unladylike. When riding a mule, women rode sidesaddle style so that long dresses hid their petticoats and ankles. An "upping block" was necessary in the front yard to help the women mount a mule or horse. Many times it was a tree stump left with roots in the ground. A sidesaddle was among the Walker-family items now in storage.

Sleds were much easier and less expensive to build than wagons or buggies. Mountain men used two bent sourwood runners, nails or pegs, and a flat board to build a sled within minutes. Using oxen (neutered bulls) to pull these sleds served well for farm work or for travel.

For longer trips, most families owned a wagon, pulled by a horse or mule. I do not know of any of our hill folk who owned a barouche, a four-wheel fancy carriage with two inside seats facing each other. However, we could quickly turn our family farm wagon into one within minutes. We installed a driver's seat and strait-back chairs in the wagon bed. The only thing it did not have was the portable top or cover.

As cars became more prevalent, they sometimes encountered the wagons. While en route home from a funeral at Elkmont, a car ran into the tailgate of our wagon-turned-barouche. No one was injured, but I believe there may have been some damage to the car radiator.

Today it is hard for us to imagine mountain folk who had never seen or heard of a car seeing one for the first time. My husband's parents, Bruce and Ida Myers, told about the first car that came through Wears Valley one evening. A few residents who saw the car lights became hysterical believing the world was ending. Mr. and Mrs. Myers described the event as if the story was true.

Somewhat less reliable is a story that one man, seeing his first car, believed it was some kind of strange animal. He then shot at it. The driver of the car stopped and ran into the woods. When asked if he killed the strange beast, the man with the rifle said he didn't know. "But," he said, "It turned the man loose that it was holding." Someone said never to let the truth interfere with a good story, which may be true in that case.

Despite having no car, the Walker Sister's saw more of the outside world than most people would believe. Jim Shelton, Caroline's husband, took them on many trips. Almost every year they attended their church's conferences held in various towns in Tennessee, and they often visited their uncle Charlie in Jefferson City, Tennessee. Martha did domestic work for families near their home and agreed to spend the night in case of illnesses. She would sometimes be away from home for three or more weeks at a time. Before the Great Depression of the late 1920's and early 1930's, Hettie worked in Knoxville at one of the hosiery mills. She boarded with her sister, Caroline, who also worked at the mill. However, the Depression sent them back home.

With no phones in the mountains, communication was a constant problem. In addition to the news Mr. Walker obtained at the local store during his lifetime, the Walker Sisters learned of the outside world by newspapers, mail, and close friends who visited them. The Walker Sisters never subscribed to newspapers or magazines as neighbors and guests supplied them with all of those. Until the Walker Sisters were left alone in the Park, devoted family members came quickly when one of the girl's blew the hunting horn signaling that they needed help.

The first mail carriers traveled on foot, then later on horseback. In more remote sections, the carrier stopped at the crest of the mountain and signaled with a bugle that the mail had arrived. Then family members rushed to meet him to receive their mail. The Walker family never had mail delivery service to their door. Rather they, as well as other families, walked approximately one half mile to Katy Hollow for their mail. To address an envelope was described as "backing" it. "Here, back this letter for me" was a common request to someone who had good penmanship.

I easily recall when the Rural Free Delivery began around 1928. Our mailing address was RFD # 15, Sevierville, Tennessee. As I recall Crockett Maples delivering our mail while riding his horse by our place. The RFD broke down the isolation and allowed us to order from Sears & Roebuck and Montgomery Ward catalogs.

At first, many families were very skeptical of ordering from the catalogs. However, Sears wrote letters telling them if they were unhappy with a choice, they could return it at no expense. Families soon gained confidence that it was safe to order by mail. Faced with a large number of catalogs to deliver, one carrier threw them in a lake. That lake was later drained to uncover his crime.

THE COMING OF THE PARK

In 1926, Congress passed a bill authorizing the establishment of a National Park in portions of Tennessee and North Carolina. The first office for this park was located in the post office in Maryville, Tennessee. It was moved to Gatlinburg in January 1940. One must read about the bitter knock-down-drag-out fights to understand the unbelievable obstacles and political chicanery that occurred. A fistfight actually took place in the House of the Tennessee Legislature. One Cades Cove resident warned if officials came again to take his property, "They would spend the next night in hell!" In 1931, Governor Horton finally signed a bill allowing condemnation of properties to create the Great Smoky Mountains National Park.

The Rockefeller Foundation donated $5 million to begin purchasing the land as a memorial to Laura Spellman Rockefeller. Then local residents raised an additional $12 million to pay all the landholders for their land. For example, my family received $12,000 for our 363 acres.

In 1933, properties for the Park remained for purchase, but all the money was spent. President Roosevelt was instrumental in getting $1,550,000 to complete the project. Records I have seen showed that all park land was purchased by 1939, but subsequent incidents regarding the Walker Sisters' land proved that information incorrect.

Residents, anxious to sell their property or to determine a purchase price, approached appraisers responsible for buying the land in the Park. Because a good spring, their chief water supply, was one of the greatest assets of any farm, farmers told appraisers many times, "be sure to see my spring." This was to make sure the appraiser know the true value of the property.

Others residents may have been eager to sell, but the Walker Sisters refused. In 1939, a Mr. Myers (first name unknown) from the National Park Service in Washington D.C. came to their home and insisted they sell their property. They flatly refused his offer. Apparently, they could not agree on a price. They first asked $15,000. Mr. Myers suggested that they consult with lawyers and family members. They informed him they did not intend to talk with anyone "as nobody knew as much about what the place was worth as they did." They later reduced their price two or three times, but they always asked to reserve a life estate.

The only other Park resident of whom I am aware who continued to reside permanently in the Park was Lem Ownby. Perhaps a book should be written of his life as well. He was blind and lived alone on his 44-acre farm on Jakes Creek in Elkmont until his death at nearly 100 years old in January 1984. He resented what had happened to his neighbors in the Park. Although he did not become as famous as the Walker Sisters, he also had many visitors from all over the world.

Two visitors were Supreme Court Justices Potter Stewart and Harry Blackmun, who were attending a conference in Gatlinburg. Their host, Foster D. Arnett, knocked on Mr. Ownby's door and explained that he had two very distinguished gentlemen, who wanted to meet him. Mr. Ownby asked if they were from Washington. When he learned that they were, he refused to meet them. He said, "I don't want to talk to them. Let them go back to Washington." Justice Blackmun and Justice Stewart were quite amused. When Mr. Arnett, who was humiliated by the incident, returned the next week for a visit, Mr. Ownby asked, "Them fellers from Washington with you?"

As the sisters remained in their home, circumstances around them changed dramatically. Their neighbors and relatives began to move; construction projects to build roads, trails, and offices commenced. Members of the 1933 Civilian Conservation Corps (CCC), part of Roosevelt's New Deal program, were stationed in the Park to complete these projects. Members of the CCC lived in temporary camps set up to house them as they worked. While creating 500 miles of hiking and horseback trails as well as bridges and campgrounds we continue to enjoy today, the CCC gave jobs to 4350 men during the height of the Great Depression.

However, politics of the time had a great impact on local events. There were so few Democrats that people joked, "Let's work hard this week so we can go to Sevierville Saturday to see a Democrat." In 1930 there were only three Democrats registered in Sevierville, Tennessee. Because my husband's father, William "Bruce" Myers, and his grandfather, Mack Myers, who lived in Wears Valley, had to travel to Sevierville to vote in the Democratic primaries, it could well be that they were two of the three. During the hiring for CCC camp work, the story circulated that officials would only consider Democrats for employment. Bruce obtained a CCC job, which saved his farm from foreclosure during the Depression. Perhaps it was because he was a Democrat.

Like nearly everyone else in the area, John Walker remained a strong Republican throughout his life. He cast his first presidential vote for Abraham Lincoln. He taught his family the virtues of the Republican Party. However, none of the Walker Sisters ever voted. Even with only one party, elections could be very contentious and sometimes very corrupt. Politicians and their supporters used money and whiskey to buy votes. It was reasonably common for supporters of a candidate to stand outside a polling place handing out silver dollars to voters who agreed to vote for their candidate.

Cloth was also used to buy votes. Before women could vote, politicians sometimes gave men cloth for new dresses for their wives. When women began to vote, politicians went straight to them. I was amazed to hear tape recordings of some of the older people telling how politicians bought votes. Someone asked an older politician how he was able to buy entire sections of votes when voters never saw him in one area. His reply was, "Men love darkness rather than light."

Even years later, my husband and I were part of the political discord in the area. I was a Republican. Everyone I knew was a Republican. In fact, during my childhood Sevier County was perhaps 99% Republican. As I grew up, I heard only unpleasant things about Democrats. My husband used to laugh that I married the first Democrat I ever met. When our old cat had kittens, he quickly announced that the kittens were Republicans. When I asked him why, he said, "Because they don't have their eyes open!" After a few years of canceling each other's votes, we both joined the same political party.

The opening of the Great Smoky Mountains National Park in the 1930's altered the lives of the citizens of this region within a single generation. Change did not come evenly. Even the most isolated farmers tried to cling tenaciously to the old ways. The coming of millions of visitors from all over the world improved and disrupted a pleasant and predictable way of life. Life for the Walker Sisters remained very much the same except that their neighbors moved away.

The formation of the Park significantly changed my own family. I have many memories of this time. My father surveyed many of the local parcels of land before acquisition of the properties began. I helped my dad plat or graph many plots he had surveyed to "prove" his work. If the degrees were all correct, it would close at 360 degrees. I cannot say positively that I worked on Park properties, but I was 10 or 12 years old when he finished surveying. Therefore, I can safely assume I was involved in the project.

Tennessee and North Carolina were in competition to acquire land for the Park. In Tennessee were 1369 parcels of land; North Carolina had only 312. The donated money went to the state that delivered good and acceptable deeds to the commission first. The state used the donated money to compensate landowners. My father worked tirelessly assisting in acquisition of the 1369 parcels of land purchased in Tennessee.

The project was very complicated. Many little Tennessee mountain farms had only homemade deeds calling for natural objects that no longer existed. Surveys of all the properties were required before sales were completed. One piece of church property in Cades Cove, which a landowner had deeded to "Almighty God," caused considerable problems. According to the book by Randolph, the Park still does not own the property.

A story is told about a man who knew the property was deeded to God. A Park ranger found him trespassing on the property. When the ranger told him he was trespassing, the man told the Ranger to proceed with charges. According to the story, Park officials told the Ranger he could not arrest the trespasser. Mr. Lendel Abbott, who had the deed, told me this story.

Directions to this property reportedly owned by "Almighty God" are: Drive the Loop Road in Cades Cove. About midway around the Loop Road, turn on to Hyatt Lane. Go across the valley to the Loop Road on the other side. Turn back to the left when reaching that road. Shortly after turning, you will see church property on the right side of the road. This is the Lawson cemetery. A man named Lawson made the deed to Almighty God.

They needed many crews to survey the land. Workers once said anyone able to carry the dumb end of a chain was hired. Some survey crews boarded in our home while doing this work. I recall a huge circle of people sitting around the living room fireplace at night telling bear, panther and snake tales before bedtime. One of my brothers overheard the term "springing" to describe a pregnant cow. One of the surveyors staying at our house had what we called a beer belly. Later, my brother remarked, "Charlie, you look like you are "springing." We never forgot that innocent comment.

Colonial David Chapman, who suffered a black eye, a missing front tooth and cracked ribs, spent many years in arduous and even life-threatening work on the project. Someone asked him if he had known what great obstacles he would encounter, what he would have charged to help develop the Park. His reply was, "There was not that much money!" It is appropriate that Chapman Highway leading to the Smoky Mountains National Park linking Knoxville to Sevierville was named in his honor.

In 1933, we left our 363-acre home in the Park and reluctantly moved to Pigeon Forge, Tennessee. Unlike our family, the Walker Sisters remained.

PRESIDENT ROOSEVELT---A WELL-KEPT SECRET

Long-time employees of The Great Smoky Mountain National Park, now deceased, are supposed to have said, "The Great Smoky Mountain National Park was President Roosevelt's New Sanctuary!" He was certainly instrumental in establishing this beautiful natural preserve. It appears that he did more than what we were generally aware.

An incident regarding President Franklin Delano Roosevelt and the Walker Sisters, a well-kept secret for over 60 years, should now be ripe for the telling. On September 2, 1940, President Roosevelt came to Gatlinburg, Tennessee to dedicate the Great Smoky Mountains National Park. I had graduated from Pi Beta Phi High School the previous May and was working at the New Gatlinburg Inn as a waitress. We left our duties in the restaurant to see the President.

It was a perfect day. The sun was shining beautifully and the weather was delightful. People lined the streets as far as we could see. I was standing on the sidewalk, within six feet of President Roosevelt when his open-top limousine very slowly passed through. He was sitting in the right rear seat of the limousine on his way to the ceremony to dedicate the Park.

After the dedication ceremony, we heard that President Roosevelt rode to Knoxville for lunch. A man, who participated in the incident, stated that Roosevelt did not go to Knoxville. He said a stand-in rode in the limousine where President Roosevelt had sat. Either the hat FDR was wearing or a duplicate was placed on the stand-in's head. The driver then went on to Knoxville so that Roosevelt could go somewhere else.

According to this guard, President Roosevelt visited the Walker Sisters during this time. Deputies of Sevier, Knox, Blount and perhaps other counties took their stations along the roads leading to the Walkers' home. Secret Service officials ordered the guards to allow only four cars to go to the Walker home. They also strongly cautioned the deputies not to reveal this visit until after Roosevelt's death.

It is quite remarkable that those deputies kept that secret all these years. However, the fact that the individual who told me about it did not want his name revealed explains some of the reason. The story has, however, been confirmed by a family member and a close family friend who remembered hearing about the visit.

The entourage, including Roosevelt, reportedly stayed approximately an hour. I have found no written record or the purpose of the visit. We will probably never know if Roosevelt just wanted to meet some crusty little old ladies who had bucked the U.S. Government for fourteen years or if he discussed the sale of their property to the government.

Four months later, on January 22, 1941, the Walker Sisters sold their 122.8 acres for $4750 to the National Park Service. When the Sisters sold their property, the stated reason was that they faced condemnation proceedings. However, the Condemnation Act, as passed by the Tennessee Legislature, expired in 1936.

Another puzzling part of the agreement giving the sisters the right to live on the property the balance of their lives allowed them to cut firewood and use the land as they needed. This agreement was very unusual. Our family and the other families were told if we stayed, we would be unable to make any changes to the land or to cut any wood on the property.

This provision would have made it virtually impossible for us or the other families to remain.

I find it fascinating that the Famous Walker Sisters, who from 1926 until after the dedication of the Park in 1940, refused to sell their 122.8 acres of land. Now just four months after President Roosevelt is supposed to have visited them, they closed the deal.

TODAY

My last visit to the Walker Sisters' home site was in 1997. The Park Service has kept the home, barn, and springhouse in excellent repair. Tourists are welcome to visit. To reach the site, drive U. S. Highway 321 (Little River Gorge Road) to the historic Little Greenbriar School House near the Metcalf Bottoms picnic area. From the schoolhouse, one can walk the old road approximately one mile to the Walker family home.

The Great Smoky Mountain National Park Service purchased the Walker Sisters' furnishings and personal belongings from their heirs, and they are now in storage in the Park. I understand that someday the artifacts will be displayed in a museum located at Occonaluftee Visitors Center in North Carolina. I do not understand why they would not be displayed in this area near their home in Tennessee.

The list of 151 items in storage includes: a buggy, a sidesaddle and blanket, 2 cotton gins, looms, a spinning wheel, a flax wheel, tan bark wagon frame, many baskets, and boxes with miscellaneous smaller items. The list also includes a fox and dinner horn they used to call sisters from the fields or summons help from neighbors. There is no mention of clothing items such as dresses or shoes.

The Walker Sisters were picturesque to be sure. They were considered old fashioned. However, there was an air about them. Maybe it was their independence. Maybe it was their focus on the basics of life, their communion with all of nature. They saw that love and laughter really exist. With all the fresh fruits, nuts, vegetables, and meats, they lived in a paradise - a Garden of Eden.

The Walker Sisters represent many of the inhabitants of this region. Of course, those dirt roads, sleds, buggies and wagons have now been replaced with modern cars and cell phones. This region, once shunned, is now the most visited in all the United States. Adjoining areas are gaining population faster than nearly any other in the country. This land, once described as inhabited by wild fierce people, has been discovered to have charm and originality. These isolated mountain people possessed a wealth of knowledge that transcends mere book learning. They were deeply religious.

Yes, we are set apart by our dialect, customs, and character. Our speech still has an old-world flavor; "quare" (for queer) is a term sometimes used. Locals may dub any newcomer a "furriner" or a flatlander. However, it would be hard to find a kinder, gentler group of people anywhere in the world.

Unlike some of the pictures painted of people in this region, the Walker family did not hold a gun on you while asking your name. They chose to remain with a life style that was best for them. We chose to move on with all the new inventions and what we call progress. We have timesaving gadgets and instant communication. But, for what? A topsy-turvy stressed-out world often filled with crime, terror and hate.

Who can say who is the loser?

IMPORTANT WALKER FAMILY DATES

John N. Walker, father, born March 3, 1841, died April 23. 1921.

Margaret Jane King Walker, born July 18, 1846, died Jan. 15, 1909

Margaret and John were married on March 29, 1866.

James Thomas Walker, born Feb. 22, 1867. Died ?

William Wylie Walker, born Sept. 2, 1868, died Feb. 5, 1929.

Margaret Jane Walker, born Aug. 29, 1870 died Dec. 20, 1962.

John Henry Walker, born Oct. 20, 1872, died Dec. 6, 1942.

Mary Elizabeth (Polly) Walker, born Feb. 6, 1875, died June 14, 1945

Martha Ann Walker, born July 8, 1877, died July _?, 1952?

Nancy Melinda Walker born Jan. 31, 1880, died July 2, 1931

Louisa Susan Walker, born Dec. 23, 1882, died July 13, 1964

Sarah Caroline Walker Shelton, born Feb. 6, 1886, died Feb. 5, 1988.

Hettie Rebecca Walker, born July 4, 1889, died Dec. 24, 1947.

Giles Daniel Walker, born Oct. 10, 1891, died April 18, 1971.

SOURCES

Burns, Inez. 1952. *Settlement and Early History of the Coves of Blount County, Tennessee* in The East Tennessee Historical Society's Publications. No. 24 : Knoxville, TN.

Callahan, North. *Smoky Mountain Country.*

Dykeman, Wilma & Stokley, Jim. 1978. *Highland Homeland, The People of the Great Smokies.* Washington, D.C., U.S. Dept of the Interior.

Greeve, Jeannette. S., reprinted 1964 by Marion R. Mangrum. *The Story of Gatlinburg.* Brazos Printing Co., Inc., Gatlinburg, TN.

Smoky Mountain Convention & Visitors Bureau. 2004. *Walker Sisters' Cabin is Monument of Heritage.*
http://www.smokymountains.org/other/media_view.html?news_id=21

Jenkins, Ralph, 1996. *Cherokee Trail of Tears: Other Paths.*
http://www.tngenweb.org/cherokee_by_blood/trail.htm

Madden, Robert R., *Walker Sisters Home Furnishing Study: Historical Data Section*, Great Smoky Mountain National Park.

Ridings, Galdys Oliver. *Cades Cove and Parts of the Great Smoky Mountains.*

Shields, A. Randolph. *The Cades Cove Story.* The Great Smoky Mountain Natural History Association

Weals, Vic. 1991. *Last Train to Elkmont.* Knoxville, TN, Olden Press.

INDEX OF PEOPLE, PLACES AND EVENTS

LOUISA'S POEMS

MY MOUNTAIN HOME
(original spelling revised)

By Louisa Walker

There is an old weather beaten house
That stands near a woods,
With an orchard near by it
For almost one hundred years it has stood.

It was my home in infancy
It sheltered me in youth
When I tell you I love it
I tell you the truth.

For years it has sheltered me
By day and by night
From the summer suns heat
And the cold winters blight.

But now the park commissioners
Come all dressed up so gay
Saying this old home of yours
We must now take away.

They coax and they wheedle
They fret and bark,
Saying we must have this place
For a national park.

For us poor mountain people
They don't give a care,
But must have a home for
The wolf the lion and the bear.

But many of us have a title
That is sure and will hold
To the city of peace
Where the streets are pure gold.

There no lion in its fury
Those paths ever trod
It is the city of peace
In the presence of God.

When we reach the portals
Of glory so fair
The wolf cannot enter
Neither the lion or the bear.

And there no park commissioner
Will ever dare
To disturb or molest
Or take our homes from us there.

GREENBRIAR CHURCH AND SCHOOL HOUSE

My father and other men met
In this valley years ago
To build a house for church and school
Where their children could go.

They cut logs in the forest
Through they had no sawmill
They were pulled by oxen
Near the foot of the hill

Yes, they all met out
With one accord
To build a house where they
Could meet to worship the Lord.

Though the building of this
house I did not see
Because the school house
Is older than me.

But I can remember
In my life's early day
How the people would meet
There to sing and pray

And preachers then spoke
Of a city grand
And a mighty happy meeting
In the promise land.

Most all the builders of the school house
Has gone on to God
Let us never forget this labor
Nor the path which they trod.

UNTITLED

The wild flowers are blooming
And the shrubs too
The ground is covered
With moss and violets too.

Haze covers the mountains
There are many a dark day
The rainbow appears
The haze rolls away.

The birds and the butterflies
Dwell amid the trees
And it's a wonderful home
For the honeybees.

The smoke from the city
Often covers the mountain too
And scatters over the trees
Making them look blue.

Some think of the mountains
As a kind of retreat
From the crowded cities
With its noisy streets.

But to me it's a quiet
peaceable dorm
The place I have always
Made my home.

NO ONE TO WELCOME ME
By Effie Shelton Phipps
after the death of
Louisa Susan Walker

I wandered back again today
To the old log cabin once more
There was no "Visitor's Welcome" sign
Hanging outside the door.

Tho tacked upon the door, now closed
A printed sign I read
'Property of the U.S. Government
No trespassing" it said.

There was no friendly "Hello"
No welcome smile so sweet
Bidding me to come inside
And rest my weary feet.

Only silence greeted me
No gaiety or laughter
Only the chirp of a katydid
Perched upon a rafter.

The old corn crib that once was full
Stands empty there today,
The old stock barn and dryhouse too
Have both been torn away.

The spring where once we quenched our thirst
On a hot summer's day
The path was overrun with weeds
No flowers bloomed by the way.

No blue smoke from the chimney curled
everywhere cobwebs clung
Upon the door that once open stood
A large padlock was hung.

No bonnets hung on the wooden peg
In the logs of the kitchen wall
No aroma from the kitchen came
No welcome mealtime call.

I walked around to the garden gate
Where once was planted seeds,
The gate upon its hinges sagged,
The plot o'er grown with weeds.

I bowed my head in silence there,
My eyes were filled with tears
Could this be the same old house
Where I had come for years?

The windows they were boarded up
I couldn't see inside
I longed so much to open the door
And view the old hearthside.

Where once the family gathered round
So snug by the fire's warm glow
While snowflakes beat on the window pane
And the wintry winds would blow.

O where are my friends of yesterday
Who once kept the hearthside warm
The hands that tilled the fertile soil
On this old rocky farm.

Their bodies lie in deep repose
Upon a windswept hill
Where zephers sweep at evening tide
And the whippoorwills call so shrill.

They are resting there in peaceful sleep
Undisturbed by mortal sound
Waiting the resurrection day
When Gabriel's trumpet shall sound.

Then they'll move to a cabin on high
And be happy for ever more
Where no doors will be closed
Or padlocks hung
On heaven's golden shore

Printed in the United States
65583LVS00002B/174